Ronit Jan Kletter

Producer & International Distributor
eBookPro Publishing
www.ebook-pro.com

When Life Gives You Lemons
Ronit Jan Kletter

Translation from Hebrew: Zoe Jordan

Contact: ronit.author@gmail.com

ISBN 9798667534402

For Assaf, Yotam and Saar, my loves.
You are the foundation of my strength.

For Yael, my pillar. Without you I would not
have found my way.

When LIFE Gives You LEMONS

RONIT JAN KLETTER

Preface

I never thought I would get cancer. It's just not something that ever crossed my mind. Getting sick is a part of life, just as all of us eventually will get old and die. But we don't think about it consciously every day; it just is one of many considerations that have become part of our subconscious. If we were to constantly think about all the things that could make us ill or kill us, we would most likely be so paralyzed by fear that we wouldn't be capable of living productive lives. So, ignoring the possibility of death is a survival mechanism, an existential necessity, which provides us with the capacity to exist in the world without the need – or desire – to consider morbidity.

Before cancer, if someone were to ask me how I was

most afraid of dying, I would have automatically said "in a plane crash," Unlike a car crash, which happens quickly, giving you little time to be afraid or think, in a plane crash, you would probably spend a certain amount of time in a state of panic and helplessness. You would have time to think about the very things hidden in your subconscious for a reason.

The very moment when you find out you have cancer, is very similar to the moment when the pilot informs the passengers that there is a malfunction and the aircraft is out of control. All you feel is fear and your only thought is: "I'm going to die." And even if you take comfort in the hope that maybe you'll survive, the fear of being stranded alone in the middle of nowhere, on water or land, could be hard to bear. So many thoughts, emotions and feelings streaming through your body at one time; it's hard to imagine.

The moment the doctor told me that the aircraft of my life had a serious malfunction, I immediately thought: "I'm going to die." I lost control. I cried. I cried for my children who would lose their mother so young. I cried for my own life, which would be cut short at such a young age. I cried for everything that I had accomplished and that I had yearned to do. More than anything, I felt disbelief that my plane was going down - after all, having cancer is unimaginable.

At first, I thought I was completely alone, even though I was surrounded by family and friends. I felt that this was happening just to me, that I alone had won this grim lottery and that I had been dealt a terrible hand.

There is nothing good about coping with breast cancer, or any cancer, but knowing that there is a way out, that it is possible to heal, can make you stronger and give you hope. And it is that hope, which I experienced alongside all the difficulties, that I wish to offer you in this book. I want you to know that you are not alone, that all of us have bleak thoughts and unbearable moments, and that even when it looks like it's impossible to go on, we can. Here's to recovery.

Yours, Ronit.

One last moment of uncertainty
a moment in which I am both
positive and negative

I embody all the possibilities
and at the same time
none of them.
A paralyzing moment
that I can't sustain
nor put to an end.
Certainty is equally scary.

*Written in the doctor's waiting room, moments
before receiving the biopsy results.

December 12, 2017

My Left (breast) is not Right

Until two weeks ago, I was a regular woman. The kind of woman that spends her time building a rewarding career, a happy, functioning home, with her family and children. My main concern was my father, who was recently diagnosed with cancer.

I had two eyes, two ears, a nose, and a long list of healthy organs that make up my healthy body.

Now I have two eyes, two ears, a nose, a long list of organs that make up my body, and one cancer that loves breasts.

Nothing prepared me for that unexpected moment when everything that I had thought was a sure thing in my life suddenly wasn't. The news of my breast cancer shattered both my illusion of control over all that exists in my own life and in others, and any perceived or real stability that had existed in my life before that moment shook me to my core.

My husband, Assaf, came with me to get the results of the biopsy two days ago. We both left work early and sat impatiently in the corridor, waiting to enter the doctor's office. I examined the people around me, wondering what they were here for, and whether I, too, would be able to leave the clinic and continue my life as usual.

When the office door opened, we jumped up and went in. A big, involuntary smile spread across my face when I saw the doctor. To this day, I do not know what possessed me to smile like that.

"From your smile, I take it we have good news," he said, grinning back at me.

"You tell me," I volleyed back. "You've got the results."

We sat across from him, my heart beating inside my chest like the sound system in a nightclub heavy on the bass. He stared at the computer screen, reading the results from my file while I tried to figure out the results from his face.

He looked serious.

After a few minutes too many, he said slowly, with a troubled expression on his face, "Well, we found tumor cells."

My hand gripped Assaf's and he squeezed mine back. It felt like we were in free fall together.

I couldn't speak. I was in shock. All I could do was weep.

The doctor laid his hand on my other hand, which was gripping the table. My head slumped, as if I had taken blow to the head from a heavyweight boxer.

"You'll get through this," he said in a comforting voice.

"I'm 37!" My anguished voice came from a place of fear and disbelief.

"I have two little boys; one is three and the other is eight. They are too young to lose their mother!" I cried, as though it were his fault.

"Just this week I operated on a 33-year-old woman with three children and she's going to be okay." He tried again to be encouraging.

"Great, so she won." My tone was sarcastic.

I felt Assaf's hand on my back, trying to support me so I wouldn't collapse on the spot. We were given instructions to take the biopsy results to the hospital for further treatment.

We left the doctor's office. I couldn't see or hear anything. Everything around me moved in slow motion and seemed surreal. All I wanted was to get out of the office building. The moment I was outside and in the fresh air,

I began weeping loudly, with short, anxious breaths. I sat, huddled on a bench, and just cried.

I called my sister and told her. She already knew about the biopsy. My parents did not. I hadn't wished to burden them. I was worried it would be too much and had hoped the results would come back negative. I asked her to come to our parents' house so we could tell them together while Assaf went to pick up the kids.

We met outside their house and discussed how to tell them. I cried again. My sister hugged me, "You'll be okay, I'll help with whatever you need," she said.

"Will you take care of my kids if I die?" I asked her. "You'll help Assaf raise them?" The tears wouldn't stop.

"I'm here," she told me. "And you'll be here, too," she added with certainty.

"How can you be so sure?" I asked her, bewildered.

"I'm an optimist by nature."

I wiped the tears from my cheeks, took a few deep breaths and we knocked on the door. We entered together, sat down in the living room, and asked them to sit as well. They were baffled by the formality.

"I didn't tell you this, but ten days ago I did a breast biopsy after the doctor found an abnormality," I said in the most nonchalant voice I was able to muster. "I had hoped that I could save you the worry and that it would come back fine, but unfortunately the results were positive," I went on in a matter-of-fact voice.

They said nothing.

I saw the shock on their faces. Mom was holding back her tears and Dad immediately started asking practical questions like, "Do you know if you'll need chemotherapy? Let's hope not..."

In a carefree tone I told them, "These days, they even have pills, you don't always have to do chemo. We'll see what the doctors say." I went on babbling about how everything is so advanced these days and that most women recover, but my mother was biting her lip.

"What's wrong, mom?" I asked her lightly, as though I had not just told her a moment ago that her daughter has cancer.

She let out a restrained cry, "You have cancer, he has cancer."

I started laughing, "This is great! We can go to treatments together, Dad and me. We'll drive to the hospital and everyone will go to their respective floor. It'll be nice..."

Mom waved her hand at me dismissively, as if to say, "how can you laugh at this," but I saw that she wasn't crying anymore and knew that my attitude had the right effect.

Strangely enough, I came out of there feeling stronger.

***

That night, when I got into bed, I felt like the sky was caving in on me. I couldn't get the image of my sweet, small children out of my mind, deprived of their mother, holding hands, asking for me but I'm not there. I finally managed to close my eyes for three hours, until reality crept into my dreams and woke me up. My mind was a busy freeway of thoughts: what needs to be organized around the house; who needs to be updated; who eats what; and a timetable of extracurriculars for each of the boys. I must not forget to inform the grade schoolteacher and the preschool teacher and the counselor and the psychologist... my head was buzzing with an endless list of tasks.

I began the morning of the shortest day of 2017 with puffy eyes and a line from a song by the band Mashina running over and over through my head: "Feels like an accident, but still acting normal." It's an ingenious line that I had never paid attention to before.

With the end of the Hanukkah holiday and the triumph of light over darkness, I will be like our planet, Earth – from the darkest day of the year, I will grow and transform and hold the light within me, each day a little more. And maybe by summer solstice, the longest day of the year, I can declare victory in this battle, or even this war. One thing is certain, I must be victorious.

I understand what I'm fighting for here. This isn't about looks, tits or hair. I'm fighting for my life and getting to see my kids grow up.

I must become a lioness. There's no other way. Cancer is a lot to digest. I am sure I haven't digested it fully. And maybe that is the way to approach it, one bite at a time, so I don't choke.

December 24, 2017

Get Out of My Veins

Today was a day of needles.

They felt like tiny daggers stabbing into me, trying to learn more about this enemy that is lining up its battalions inside my body. I hope that future needles will contain deadly poison to annihilate the invader to its very core.

Yesterday, I said I was fighting. I was practicing courage of the mind. Today, I had to demonstrate courage of the body.

It hurt but I said nothing.

I dashed from one test to another, starting with another biopsy, this time of the lymph nodes in my axilla, or armpit. I proceeded to a PET-CT scan to assess how much the disease had spread. They cut me and stabbed me, and I promised myself I would not make a fuss; this was the real war. To say that I'm going to defeat this cancer is not lip service; I must fight it by tolerating the pain and being resilient physically, as well as mentally.

I don't know how to scream when I'm in pain. I usually grit my teeth, bite my lips, or clench my fists until my fingernails pierce my flesh. When I gave birth, even the doctor in the delivery room asked me why I didn't scream when it hurt. He said it helps with the contractions, but I couldn't. I can only scream in anger.

And for some reason, I'm not angry.

Maybe it has yet to come; they say this process has many phases.

I sat in the prep room with other cancer patients like myself, each drinking a jug of contrast material as though it were a tea party. Occasionally, in that atmosphere of shared destiny and exchanging notes, interesting small talk developed. It was so strange and disconnected from the life I had had just a few days ago, but also natural and human, at that most basic level. I enjoyed listening to them, realizing once again how everyone is a world unto himself, and how none of us know what tomorrow will bring.

The last person to enter the room before me was an older man with colon cancer; he had had many surgeries and even showed me the scar. If he were younger and I were blonder I would have felt as though I were in the movie "Lethal Weapon." But he observed me and could tell I was new at this, although I hadn't said a word. He just looked at me and said, "You need a lot of strength to fight this. Don't stop and don't give up. Even if there are situations where you feel like there's a knife at your throat, nothing is lost yet, there's a way out of that, too."

I don't know if it was the contrast material, the pain from the biopsy, or maybe the long fast that infused me with such spirituality but I felt that something in him; this man who chose life, had been sent to give me a message of strength.

I entered the exam room and as the iodine was being pumped into my vein, which felt as though it might burst, I closed my eyes, breathed deeply, and remembered his words. They helped me not to fear the pain that had only just begun.

December 26, 2017

Family Photos

This morning I set aside some quality time with my dad.

We've always had things in common and now more than ever. We sat together and found ourselves leafing through a binder of oncology patients' rights, comparing the biopsies we'd each had. I don't have his kind of cancer nor does he have mine so we're both learning what the other is going through. We discussed the similar tests we had and he told me what to expect from tomorrow's MRI. I wondered to myself which vein would turn blue this time.

My father is a courageous man. He's been through wars and is full of life wisdom, so I was surprised to discover that he, like me, had also found the insertion of iodine for the PET-CT scan incredibly painful. It occurred to me that if this iron man who raised me had almost cried out in pain (but refused to make a peep or the slightest movement that might botch the test) then it's fine that I complained when my vein felt as if it were about to burst. He said that in the moment when it hurt the most he thought, "this is the time to stay strong." I'd had exactly the same thought when I felt that pain.

I wondered to myself if thoughts can be passed down genetically, like cancer.

I found myself saddened by seeing family pictures of Assaf and I with the children. But I knew I wouldn't die. Not from cancer, anyway. I won't let that happen.

Still, something in those family photos, seeing us smiling on vacations with no idea what was waiting around the corner, made me think the sad thought: when will we smile like that again? We were so carefree and full of life with red cheeks flushed from a walk in the sun, full of strength and radiating with happiness.

It's hard for me not knowing when this whole journey would be over. That's probably because I was never able to delay gratification. I was born without that mechanism. I'm surprised that when they interpreted the PET-CT scan they didn't mention that it's missing from my body. My dad is like that, too. I bet that's also genetic. And even though he won't have to do chemo, we will both eventually go bald.

With going bald on my mind, I went to the hairdresser to shorten it as part of my own "prepare yourself for chemo" program.

> You start by letting go of your hair gradually,
> A little bit each time.
> You let go of the person you were until now,
> Bit by bit.
> Every curl and self-conception,
> Little by little.
> Bit by little bit.

December 30, 2017

Cancer Plays Soccer

First half - an unexpected offense

The appointments in the oncology unit had nearly left me broken, both spiritually and emotionally. The really scary thing was that nothing had really started yet. It was all testing and talking: the painful kind of tests and the depressing kinds of talk. At my first meeting with my oncologist, I came to realize that nothing was certain and that everything was going to change repeatedly. The uncertainty and the lack of control are particularly difficult for me. How can one be expected to constantly reassess the course of action?

How can one maintain stability when everything is shifting?

I had also realized that 'chemotherapy', with its 12

letters, entails taking countless pills to counteract its side effects and injections that will safeguard various organs and the immune system. As if attempting to stich up a patchwork, the medications pile up, one on top of the other, with the aim of one treating the side effects of the other. This information alone was enough to make me feel geriatric and I felt the fear seeping in, making me nauseous even before I took any of the drugs.

After these appointments, I had to undergo an MRI scan, the purpose of which was to get a clearer image of the tumor, both to determine at which stage my cancer was as well as for monitoring during chemo, and to prepare for surgery. I went into another prep room where they were supposed to give me an IV with a contrasting agent to be added to the cocktail that had already been mixing in my body for the past few days. A nice doctor asked for my arm and I extended both arms towards her. Arms which, until a week ago, had been tapping away at the keyboard at work, and were now covered with hematomas in a whole range of shades of blue and purple from all the transfusions and needles. She searched hard for a new, fresh patch of skin in which to insert the IV, trying unsuccessfully, as if my body was resisting, not wanting it, and every attempt caused fresh pain and exhausted me. Tears pooled in my eyes as I thought about my life and what had become of it.

The needle doctor left me for a moment and suddenly the director of the hospital's breast imaging unit passed by. She had met me during my battery of tests.

"How are you?" She asked me with a smile.

And, feeling all alone there, dressed in a hospital gown, sterile covers on my feet, stripped of my powers and my identity, I burst into uncontrollable tears right in front of her. I cried all my sadness outward.

She sat down beside me, placed her hand on me, and suddenly I wasn't alone.

"What happened?" She asked with interest.

"I feel like my life came to a screeching halt, that I was hit by an asteroid that knocked me off track, and I'm lost, drifting into scary black space, looking for a bright galaxy to reach for, looking for promise. Just a week ago, I was still at work, living my normal life, and suddenly I've been at the hospital every day for a week. And so many tests and jabs and so much uncertainty. And look at my arms, even my veins can't take it anymore. It's just too much for me," I said all at once.

"You are just at the beginning now, which means lots of tests, so of course everything feels scary and uncertain. Do you want me to try and put in your IV?" she asked calmly.

I nodded yes.

Skillfully and pleasantly, she inserted the IV into my vein, and earned a place in my heart.

***

Second half - recovery

The following day. Like every day lately, I woke up with the dawn, as reality crept into the relative calm of my sleep. As though my out-of-body self and I have united and immediately given birth to a sense of panic accompanied by heart palpitations and a terrible anxiety-induced nausea.

Yesterday we reached a decision about the date I will begin chemo: New Year's Day, 2018. I didn't want New Year's Eve because it's Assaf's 40th birthday. Even if we don't have a big celebration, at least we won't be spending the day at the hospital.

Today we decided to tell the kids. We can't wait any longer. The chemo will have side effects, and we won't be able to hide what's happening anymore.

The last few days, in between tests, I had consulted with every professional I could find about how to tell our children. I counted the hours until Yotam would get home from school. Assaf went to pick him up and bring him home. Before he arrived, I made some comfort food to cushion the shock of the news, schnitzel and rice. For a moment, the return to cooking and the simpler chores of life, instilled a sense of normality and comfort.

When Assaf and Yotam got home, we all sat down to eat together, and we told him that I have cancer.

I was afraid of the conversation, like the anxious feeling before an exam. I was afraid to hurt him or make him sad. I was afraid of him living in perpetual anxiety that I might die. I was afraid that he would ask me to promise him that I wouldn't die. I was afraid he would cry, shout, or act out, and that I would start crying right along with him.

I was afraid of crying while I told him as though re-telling myself that I have cancer just a week after I found out. I wrote notes to myself and then I even rehearsed to ensure that I would remember the things that were important for me to tell him. I must be calm, so my voice wouldn't tremble, to convey the belief that I will get through this.

As it turned out, he was wonderful, better than any scenario I had envisioned.

We sat across from him and told him that we had to tell him something. I began to tell him according to the speech I had memorized and when I got to the sentence,

"I have cancer," he made a face, kind of embarrassed and a little sad. In response to his reaction, my voice began to tremble. Assaf took over spontaneously, saying, "this is a kind of cancer you can recover from."

Yotam inhaled deeply and let out a *fffuuuu* sound (which means "we dodged a bullet" in kidspeak).

"In order to get better, I have to get treatment that will be really tough, and in order to really get to the cancer, it will be tough on me, too," I explained, when I felt that my voice was steady again.

"How did you get it?" he asked. "And why does it happen?"

"Nobody knows for sure," I replied.

"Ahh, I remember!" He cried, saving me from coming up with an answer, "It's a cell in the body that goes crazy and decides to split too many times."

After we got through the hard part of the conversation, he asked: "Can I tell my friends that because my mom is sick, I can't make playdates at my house?"

I marveled that he seemed to understand how things would change.

Yotam kept getting up from the dining table; he didn't seem able to stay seated. "Why did you tell me?" he suddenly asked.

"Because you are a part of the family. Things will

change at home, and it's important that you understand why, and that you be an ally in my battle against cancer," I replied.

"It's possible you could lose," he said in a worried voice.

"There are things I am not willing to lose," I said firmly. I had not prepared myself for this statement. "I'm willing to lose at soccer, or playing Clash Royale, but not to cancer. I will do everything I can to get better."

"Even head surgery?" he asked in his childish voice.

"Yes," I said.

"Even on your brain?" He tried to up the ante.

"Even that."

"Even on your butt?" He asked and grinned like he was trying to trip me up.

A big smile came across my face. "Yes. And while they're at it, maybe they can make it a little smaller." I joked.

Finally, he got up and played me two songs on the flute.

I was deeply touched.

I always had doubts about my mothering. I felt like I wasn't good enough, not like I'd have liked. But the way he behaved made it clear to me that I had done something right here.

When Saar got back from nursery school, we sat down to talk with him, too. Yotam asked to join the conversation and we allowed him to, but requested that he let us tell Saar first, and only when we were finished, he could contribute if he wanted.

I sat Saar on my knees as I held him and told him that I have cancer.

"Cancer like the SpongeBob[1] character?" he asked, and I laughed.

"It really *is* funny that they named the disease the same as the creature. But no, not like Mr. Krabs."

We explained to him that I would get treatments and feel bad, and that I wouldn't be able to be with him all the time. It didn't seem to bother him too much. Yotam waited patiently and then added, "Saar, did you know that cancer is when a cell in our body makes a mistake and starts to divide into more and more and more cells, until it makes a ball. And now Mom will get medicines and treatments to make the ball smaller."

I was amazed by his ability to explain such a complex process. And then he added: "This means that you and I won't be able to have friends over for the time being, instead we'll go to their houses. Do you understand?"

---

1   In Hebrew, as in Latin, the word for 'crab' and 'cancer' are the same (like the astrological 'cancer' sign of the zodiac)

Saar nodded sweetly, and I wondered if Yotam told him that so he would take it into consideration, or because he himself was still processing the effect on his own social life.

Yotam spent the afternoon with his best friend. When I picked him up, he immediately shared: "We talked about how maybe it would be better if at school I say you have chest cancer and not breast cancer because kids might think that the word 'breast' is kind of funny."

I smiled at him and said, "That's an interesting idea. You can choose who you tell and how you tell them, however you think is best. We have nothing to be ashamed of."

That evening, after Saar had gone to bed, Yotam was lying on the living room sofa, and I was seated beside him, by his feet, looking at him. Several hours had passed since I'd given him the news, and he asked in his sweet, heart-melting voice, "Mom, if there are treatments for this kind of cancer and you can get better, why do only 90% get better? Why doesn't the rest recover?"

"How do you know about those statistics?" I asked him in surprise.

"I read it online," he answered naturally.

I looked into the wide, intelligent eyes before me, waiting for a reply. The wheels in my brain were spinning at record speed to try and provide an answer that would be close to the truth, but not alarming.

"Maybe they discovered the cancer after it had already spread and gotten strong, or they were sick with other illnesses, too, and it was hard for their bodies to fight it," I said, considering every word.

Plus, this disease is deceptive and doesn't always give in, I added to myself.

"I know you'll beat it and win," he said firmly and seriously, as though we had switched roles for a few seconds.

"How do you know?" I asked, amazed by his confidence and at the same time worried that I wouldn't live up to his expectations.

"Because you will do whatever it takes to get better. Even if it's hard and painful, you will do it, so you'll win," he answered quickly, as though he had been born with this insight and just waited for this moment.

I did not know then how much that phrase of his would follow me in the darkest, hardest moments. As my body lay exhausted from suffering, a single memory cell from precisely this moment would wake up and inject those words into my veins and revive my limbs to get up and keep on going, despite the pain and difficulty.

All I could do then was look at him, happy and touched, my eyes moist with tears, and tell him – and myself – that he's right that now I have no choice, I am committed to success. I'm committed to him, to this intelligent, gentle boy, this little chick of mine. I will do whatever it takes to remain with him in the nest and teach him to fly and be here to see him grow up. No matter how many times I kick the ball in the first half, and no matter how many times I stumble and fall face-first into the mud. In the end, I will prevail. I must win.

I held him to me and told him that it moved me to hear him think like that, that he believes in my strength, and together, him, me and my cancer, went to play the FIFA video game.

Speak to Me in Images

I didn't know this hospital. In general, a healthy woman such as myself shouldn't be familiar with any hospitals, except maybe the maternity ward.

Well, these days it seems that that's all changed, though I must say, to this hospital's credit, they really make an effort to minimize the sterile hospital feeling and make it as comfortable and welcoming as possible.

Starting at the entrance, there's a good hotel-like smell throughout the foyer, which is decorated entirely with the work of famous painters and imbues a sense of cultural refinement, like a museum, in a moment that generally has no regard for serenity or art.

I never saw myself as a particularly artistic type. Museums always felt stifling to me (aside from natural history museums), and when abroad I always preferred to absorb the local culture in the streets. But this journey I've been sentenced to, which is all worry and fear, physical and emotional pain, made me decide that for every treatment and each stage I will choose an image that speaks to me and I will write about it.

That will be my breath of fresh air, or at least different air, from some other life: a breath of life.

FIRST
CHEMOTHERAPY
TREATMENT

I will stand firm against it
I will hang on with my claws
By my teeth
Against the upheaval of its cruel winds
Until it subsides

And I will rise up
Above its ruins.

Tiger in a Tropical Storm by Henri Rousseau 1891

January 2, 2018

Hooked up to Life

Yesterday I had my first chemotherapy session, or, as they say, "chemo."

It began with a long, increasingly anxious wait and continued with searching for a viable vein amongst the multicolored hematomas on my arms. With my first-timer privileges I got a cubicle with a window looking out and was happy to see the rain and the natural light outside. Once the vein was found and the infusion inserted, I was hooked up to various bags in different shapes and colors. Slowly, those "good" poisons dripped into me, infiltrating my body to take a swipe at my cancer.

All those hours hooked up to those bags, I felt that I had gone through a grueling marathon of hard, painful, stressful tests to get to this moment. This moment in which I would be more connected to life than to death.

It's strange to think how the conscious insertion of poison into the body can actually be welcome to the person who has something worse, something that has taken up residence inside her body, that threatens to spread.

At first, everyone receiving treatment was tucked away in their own corner, but as the hours passed, we began chatting amongst ourselves. Curtains were drawn and consultations began concerning wigs and side effects, hair loss and different types of cancer. I am always amazed by the friendships that form among people with similar troubles. I wonder if that's a human phenomenon or more of a cultural thing.

When I finished the chemo, I was so happy. I felt that this was the actual beginning of the battle that I had been waiting for since the moment of my diagnosis. I was *so* happy that I agreed to do an additional biopsy immediately afterwards: my fourth in total. Why? Because we want to know everything.

I lay there, smiling but scared. A host of radiologists, who have already seen me daily, gently, and laughingly got me through this biopsy as well. I never thought that it was possible to undergo so many medical procedures in so short a time.

My beloved Assaf's fortieth birthday celebrations were more modest than we could have imagined and tinged with sadness that we managed to banish for short stretches of time. Between the needles, the infusions and incisions, the bandages and stitches, out of those injuries and the fiery inferno, I will be reborn as a different version of myself, in the very same hospital in which Assaf was born, exactly forty years ago.

January 5, 2018

Puddles of Sadness

This sadness takes over and spreads, like cancer, to every capillary in the body, to every corner of my life.

It's Friday morning and everyone is going about their business; the world goes on turning. People run around with grocery bags and errands, and couples sit in coffee shops.

Meanwhile, I'm busy, too, with my medicine and injections and nausea. I go to the clinic, pale and faltering. Assaf holds me up the whole way so I won't fall and all around I see everyone's normal lives passing quickly before me, as I move slowly to get a shot that will strengthen my bone marrow and improve my immune system.

My arsenal of drugs comes with an abundance of side effects, but none of them indicate sadness.

The sadness of a life put on hold.

The sadness of the shift from managing life to managing illness.

The sadness of my children hurting.

The sadness of my being a burden to Assaf and to my family.

The sadness of soon becoming an aged house pet, losing hair, sprawled helplessly in some corner of the house, shrinking with the feeling of being a burden to those around me.

I hear Saar in the evenings, shouting on his way to the shower, "I want Mom! I want Mom!" Meanwhile, I'm exhausted, unable to respond to him. I lie in the bedroom, only a few meters away from him, like a wounded animal in an imaginary cage.

I hear Assaf telling him gently: "Mom can't bathe you; she's not feeling well. You remember how we said that she would take medicine that would make her feel bad?" And I feel my tears quietly trickling and my arms too weak to wipe my own wet cheeks. The rain keeps falling outside; drops of life for nature that reflect my tears.

I have so much sadness and nothing to do with it, just try to let the blessed rain do its best cleanse my grief.

To take it one storm at a time.

To try to skip through the puddles with a clumsy grace, and not wallow in the sadness.

January 8, 2018

Bad Hair Day

Today I explored the world of wigs.

I didn't think I would want one, but I figured I should consider all my options before letting go of my hair. Hair loss is probably the least significant side effect of cancer because unlike breasts, it grows back; for most people it even comes back healthier. Still, it's the first distinctive marker of cancer patients, the equivalent of coming out of the cancer closet.

At the little wig salon, I saw sparse-haired women coming for treatment that included shaving the thin hair that was left and growing irregularly, wig-fitting for new clients and shampooing and caring for the wigs of the veterans. All the salon's staff had experienced chemotherapy-related hair loss themselves and decided to give back to those whose time had come to go through this stage.

I sat waiting for my turn, observing what was going on all around. It was a shock to realize that any second now I would be one of them.

A pretty young woman came into the salon with a bag containing two braids of natural hair to donate. She didn't even want to give out her personal details to get the certificate, just to contribute. She left and came back a few seconds later to ask if they needed volunteers.

By this point, they had shaved all the thin hair off an older woman's head and I started to cry. The girl on staff at the salon thought I was crying at that sight. It took me a few seconds to manage to tell her that I was touched by these people and their actions, by all the tender-heartedness that I thought had been cancelled along with the "Care Bears" show.

It's an entire world of giving that was unknown to me. There are kind people who give of themselves on a regular basis, not in exchange for anything, just to do something good for others who are going through a hard time. I looked at the new volunteer and felt sad that all these years I was too caught up in myself and my perfect life to think of going and doing something generous for its own sake.

There were bags of knitted hats in happy, lively colors from nice grandmas all over the country, who sit and knit to clothe the exposed heads of cancer patients. There is so much love knit right into these hats. There is so much love for our fellow human beings right there inside of us. Where is all that humanity hiding when everything is alright?

I tried on wigs in different colors and styles. It was a funny, sad experience because I looked like a lot of people, just not like myself. I felt unnatural, weird, maybe even weirder than when I imagined myself bald.

The first wig I tried on was the closest in color and length to how my hair was before, and I walked over to Assaf to see how he responded.

He burst out laughing and said, "You look like Brian May."

I looked in the mirror and saw the likeness immediately. "I do!" I started laughing as he hummed "Bohemian Rhapsody."

The second wig I tried on was a different style and color. We were trying a slightly crazy look. This time, I looked at myself in the mirror first and was startled.

"I look like a serial killer or a fugitive wearing a wig in some gas station bathroom in a thriller," I told Assaf and this time it was his turn to laugh.

By then I had realized that wearing a wig was probably not for me, but I tried on another one or two just to be sure before abandoning the idea and giving in to baldness.

There was an older woman standing beside me; she had been in chemotherapy for eight months already and had not yet shaved her hair. She couldn't bring herself to do it, and her head was mostly bald with clumps of thin hair. For eight months she must have been gathering all the hairs that fell out of her head and around her house. Today she would get it over with, she declared to me as we tried on hats.

And indeed, she sat in the chair beside mine and surrendered her lonely tresses to the shaver as they dropped to the floor one by one, her eyes tearing up. Everyone watching was moved.

That same moment I realized that even if I got a wig, I wouldn't use it. The same way this woman tried but failed to deny the loss of her hair, I won't succeed either. It's part of the process and nothing to be ashamed of. The baldness is a sign of our resilience, which has been hiding under our hair all this time.

January 11, 2018

The Lion of the Mind

These are my last hours with hair.

We spent the day together.

We passed along final messages, talked, strolled together in the wind, went a little wild and finally made it work. It promised to be on good behavior before the separation, even agreed to come with me to choose scarves and hats and was humble as we tried them on.

My hair and I were in this together, even though it would soon be shaven off.

Together we arranged for a leave of absence for all the clips, scrunchies, hair pins and other accessories. We thought how weird it'll be that my hair would no longer cascade over my ears or get in my eyes in the wind.

I used to play a game with the kids where I cover them

up with my mane. They call it the hair monster. But even the hair monster will have to go on leave for a while.

Once, at lunch with a good friend, I laughed that whenever I go to sleep with wet hair, I wake up looking like a lion. Today, she came with me to choose scarves and hats and wrote me a beautiful blessing that said, "To be a lion is a state of mind, not just the state of your wild hair." I couldn't have said it better myself. Like Samson, tomorrow I will shave off my tresses, but that is not where my true resilience lies. It is in the imaginary mane that I will grow, in my faith in my ability to heal and return, roaring with vitality. I will be accompanied by Assaf and our sweet children, who will be the ones to cut my hair and share this scary moment with me in which I go from being concealed — to revealed.

January 14, 2018

G.I. Jane

It's been three days since the shaver met my head and it's hard getting used to the results.

The salon visit with the kids went better than expected. I noticed that in the rough-cut phase, with scissors, before the shaver, Yotam took over with unsettling delight. When my hair regrows, I noted to myself, I might have to keep an eye on them to make sure they don't shave my head again while I'm sleeping.

They were great though. I think the fact that they weren't concerned and that they cooperated, encouraged me not to be too shocked by the new circumstances.

But it is shocking — not the loss of hair itself, because hair grows back, but the result, which is so very strange. After all, the last time I was this bald I was a baby and it has been growing ever since.

I suppose I would get used to my new look faster if I sat in front of a mirror all day, but the truth is that when I'm around the house, I don't really feel the difference until I pass by a mirror or windowpane or find my reflection in the oven door or when the phone screen is off.

I ask my mirror image, who are you?

And in my mind what I'm really asking is, who will you be when this is all over?

When I go out, things feel different; there is a surrounding breeze on all sides and it's cold! It's the wrong season not to have my head-warming hair.

Back on the home front, each felt differently about the new me.

To Assaf — I am beautiful no matter what (let's give him the benefit of the doubt — for now).

To Yotam — I am Luis Suárez (a famous soccer player) with the potential to soon become, with the imminent baldness, Zinedine Zidane.

And to Saar — "Mommy looks like a boy."

No doubt this is what every woman wants to hear from the men in her life.

It's not easy. I don't like myself like this, but I understand that it's a small price to pay for being healthy.

And in these moments, between the baldness and headscarves, I have to choose between a butch look and a Jewish Orthodox look, and remind myself over and over that no matter which 'look' I choose, the important thing is I choose life.

The Reveal

Given how fast we scheduled the treatments, we notified our friends and family right away. But from the moment I had my head shaved, everyone else was left wondering: was this a premature mid-life crisis, or was something going on that they didn't know about?

Should we tell the neighbors? I wondered. On the one hand, it seemed weird to stop them on the stairs and tell them something like that. Would I just say, "I have cancer" out of the blue? On the other hand, it's already quite conspicuous — I'm bald or wearing headscarves, not saying anything may be even weirder. There's never a good time for telling people and since Assaf and I had enough on our plates, we decided not to make a decision.

Each person we did choose to tell, dealt with the news

in their own way. There were those who sent messages offering help with groceries, with the kids, anything we might need. There was a neighbor who came to our house with a cake in her hands and tears in her eyes, inquiring after my health and offering to help with anything and everything. Then there were those who ignored what was happening, those that saw but ignored it, and those that didn't even notice.

I'd been told to be prepared for different responses from different people; a person's reaction depends on their own capacity to cope. I was counseled that there would be looks of compassion and people who would cross the street, just so as not to have to face me and find the right words. It's a little like comforting someone in mourning only I'm still alive.

But despite the forewarning, there were some instances that were hard to swallow. I saw them as part of what I referred to as the "Parade of Tactlessness."

For example, a close friend from work wrote me a text with the following message: "I feel sorry for you, I'm keeping my fingers crossed." Yes. "Feel sorry." As though he felt somehow superior.

I replied: "Don't feel sorry. Sorry is not in my vocabulary just now."

On another occasion, while waiting at the airport for a

domestic flight, a work acquaintance passed by me several times. I was wearing a headscarf to cover my bald head. The first time, he acted as if he hadn't seen me. The second time, I smiled at him and he looked away. The third time, I said a feeble "hello," but he didn't answer.

There was another incident around the time I was just starting treatment. A friend from work, wishing to give me strength, sent me a link to a blog by his sister who had gotten sick and recovered. I read the blog and was truly heartened by the things she had written. But then I noticed that he had sent another link. He referred me to a new blog that she started writing when she had a recurrence of cancer, this time as a spinal metastasis. When I heard she passed away not long afterwards, at the age of 36, I was horrified. I kept thinking that even if she had recovered fully, death was waiting around the corner all that time.

Without a doubt, the prize goes to a bookstore saleswoman. Four days after we received the diagnosis, and four days before we would tell the kids, we met Yotam at the mall after a PET scan at the hospital. We went into a bookstore and, while he was looking at the Captain Underpants selection, Assaf made sure that Yotam stayed a safe distance from me so that I could ask the saleswoman with utmost discretion if they had a book about cancer I had heard about that was for kids. While she was looking for it, I added, "He doesn't know yet," and pointed at Yotam, "So please be discrete."

"We don't have that book," she told me. "Maybe it's only available on self-publishing websites."

"Thanks," I said and started to head toward Assaf and Yotam.

Suddenly, she emerged behind us without any warning, "If you want, we have other books about cancer!" She announced, nearly shouting.

I was wide-eyed with shock, gesturing to her with a finger over my lips that she keep quiet because Yotam was right there. But she leaned over him as he flipped through the books and told him in a childish voice, as though he were a toddler, "do you like sea creatures? Do you like crabs?" Assaf and I, stunned and hysterical, indicated to her to stop, but she was on a roll: "There are all kinds of creatures... there's the crab, and there are lots of other animals. What do you like?"

"Come, Yotam," Assaf swiftly pulled him away. I hurried after them, stunned and glad that Yotam was so absorbed in Captain Underpants and the innocence of childhood that he didn't even notice the saleswoman jeopardizing it.

January 15, 2018

Must be Tough

The hardest part of dealing with cancer is the uncertainty and, at the same time, the feeling of drowning; drowning in information, drowning in fear, sinking in a sea of thoughts, some of which are as clear as day, and others as dark as night. Within this sinking feeling I keep looking for something to grasp onto, like a branch, any positive snippet of information, any chance, any optimistic comment from a doctor or plan of action.

A change in plans feels like a slap in the face, leaving me red and raw and tearing up. It undermines my expectation of routine, structure, and anything stable, even if it's temporary. Each time I manage, with great difficulty, to get the tiniest hold on that branch, that chance, that action plan, a change comes along and throws me off.

And each time, once again, I scramble not to drown in my own tears, in the dark waves of menacing thoughts, grasping for something to hang onto.

Thankfully, when I feel like I've lost my senses, precisely as the fatigue of sadness exhausts my body, I manage to move my arms and reach out a little. I manage to lift myself above the waves, breathe in a little air, see that there is still a horizon, even if until now I could only see the ocean floor.

They say optimism is about looking at the glass half-full. In recent weeks, many half-full glasses have been spilled; I've seen oncology get the better of optimism. Despite that, and though I know it doesn't always help, I will strive to look through rose-colored glasses and not just because pink is the color of breast cancer.

From one treatment to the next there is uncertainty regarding effectiveness. Various strange side effects make doubts creep in and thoughts crawl deeper into the fear centers. We are so used to certainty. Increasingly, in this modern world, technology accustoms us (and evidently also poisons us) to having a sense of control. We know where people can be found at any given moment, whether they read the message we sent, and other marvels that bely our infatuation with control.

About two weeks ago, I went to a meeting at Saar's

preschool, and two parents stood outside talking loudly. The woman was mad that her husband hadn't seen her message and, as a result, he had arrived late. In his defense, he just said he was sorry and that his phone had been on silent. That notion stayed with me.

I felt like my cancer had also been on silent.

It accompanied me for some unknown period and took bites out of my life without my noticing. Even now it's on silent, just in a different way. In its current state of silence, it won't tell me if I did damage to it by delivering two liters of poison straight to its heart. It won't tell me if it's shrinking in fear or laughing in my face, stretching out its arms to show me how far it can reach. It has been and remains quiet.

As for me, I'm doing everything I can so it will leave me be. So that at the end of this journey I can find my own silent state — a quiet mind.

From my experience over the past three-and-a-half weeks, I can say that we have virtually no control over anything. It just seems like we do. The really horrible things don't announce themselves, don't know if you've seen the message, don't leave GPS markers. Our knowledge of the situation keeps changing and the plan of action must adapt along with it.

There are hard days when the black clouds darken

everything. I don't know how one makes it through. Luckily, the earth keeps on spinning and night comes each day and gives me a chance to sleep.

I've thought more than once how great it would be to go through this whole process under anesthesia. No side effects, no fear. They would look after your body while you sleep through a 'long winter,' and you would just wake up healthy. Maybe they'll figure out how to do this, say by the year 2040.

SECOND CHEMOTHERAPY TREATMENT

And on that day I awoke
to the tangle of my life;
So thick there was no light,
No hope.
Among the stubborn rocks of doubt
And tangled tree trunks
I wriggle to find a way out;
Struck and scratched
With every try.
At times I drop down
Face first into the soil,
Drenching it with my tears,
My fear,
My desperation,
My weakness.
I cry out, gasping to fill my lungs.
I will turn on my back,
See the green canopy
Of treetops,
The color of life
Shadowing me from above
All the time.

Painting by Paul Cézanne
- In the Park of the Chateau Noir - 1900

January 22, 2018

Pieces of Ronit

This story begins a week ago.

The day before the second chemotherapy treatment, I woke up in the morning to discover a swelling just above my collarbone. This very noticeable swelling was found to be a swollen lymph node, or supraclavicular node; my anxiety swelled along with it.

Unlike the person I used to be, I managed to wait the 24 hours until the treatment day, and there at the hospital, before the second round of chemo, I was examined. Because the nature of the gland could not be established with certainty, the doctors decided to take a biopsy, which is now the fifth biopsy I've undergone.

Nearly a week passed, the side effects from the chemo were merciless, yet the swelling went back from whence it came. Deep inside, I began to relax and think that maybe I got scared for nothing.

Until yesterday.

Assaf and I went to the oncology appointment for the biopsy results and like a grenade to the face — the results came back positive.

In the sea of uncertainty in which I've been swimming this past month, there was one anchor that I grasped onto — that my body was free of cancer apart from the breast and one lymph node in the armpit. It was a tree trunk to lean on. It was a relatively good starting point as it meant I had good chances of recovery. But that trunk turned out to be a thin reed that snapped in an instant and the earth trembled under my feet.

There were stuttered questions, shock, more questions. We decide to switch chemo protocol to the kind that allows for the introduction of molecularly targeted therapy immediately. Once again, I don't know what to expect; what will the new side effects be? How will I respond to this new therapy? What are the success rates?

The oncologist agreed that this is not as good as we had thought, but says we are still aiming for full recovery. Yet all I hear are doubts creeping within me: Did the treatment work? Did the cancer spread during treatment? Will this treatment work?

Today I won't take pity on you.

Today I will tell you all the dark, hard thoughts: What will happen if none of the treatments work?

How much time will I have?

And what about my children? After all, they're still so little. How can I say goodbye to them? Will I make it to Yotam's Bar Mitzvah? What about Saar's?

Yesterday, outside the maternity ward I saw a couple come out and take photographs with their newborn in the car seat before they went home. Just three-and-a-half years ago that was us with Saar. We still have a baby in the house. He's still a baby to me.

And the thoughts don't let up, they gain momentum and are at least as violent as my cancer. They hit me in all the places that hurt, and all of them involve the children.

I left the oncologist's and cried, walked down the hallway, and cried, sat with Assaf, and cried, just crying, and seeing darkness before my eyes all the while.

The darkness of being scared to death.

I can't imagine a world in which I'm not here for them but at the same time, that's all I can seem to think about.

I'm not willing to succumb to this shit. But at the same time, I feel so defeated that I want to just lie down and die this minute and be done with it. Enough already.

The nucleus of my soul has been breached and its

burning core is pouring out and burning up everything I have ever been. How many earthquakes must I survive until I can recuperate? Will the tectonic plates return to their places?

A month has passed since the diagnosis and it seems that something has been going wrong about once a week, on average. I barely manage to put myself back together before getting hit with the next debilitating thing. I can't keep up. I can't put myself back together faster than the cancer breaks me down.

I'm unable to leave the hospital. I sit in the beautiful museum-like corridor and can't stop crying. I cry for my fear, for the loss, for the doubt, for the feeling of being unable to go home and be a mother. Finally, we drive home. Evening comes on.

Feeling hollow, with all my tears gone, I went into the house. My dad was looking after Saar. I sat down beside the two of them and when Saar hugged my leg and cheered, "Mommy! Mommy!" I burst into tears. I found I had more tears, after all.

I was so emotionally depleted I couldn't protect them all anymore: my kids from watching me fall apart, my dad who, because he is coping with his own cancer, I have tried to spare from my worry over my cancer, nor Assaf.

I became a puddle.

My dad took me aside and hugged me and I cried into his shoulder. I don't remember the last time that I cried like that on my father's shoulder. There was something so healing about being embraced by my own parent. I realized how much I was withholding from myself, in my attempt to protect them from the difficulty, in my fear of burdening them.

I spent the rest of the evening alternating between crying and staring into space. I've never been so mentally broken, pulverized.

All that's left are pieces of Ronit.

January 23, 2018

Putting Humpty-Dumpty Together Again

I decided to spend the morning with my parents.

I arrived despondent, exhausted, and humbled. I allowed myself to be recharged and just be my parents' daughter. For a few hours I didn't have to be a wife or mother, fighting to stay alive for her children.

I sat in their beautiful garden amidst the birds and the bright yellow lemons and the pleasant, warm sunshine. I inhaled the air. I breathed deeply.

My dad made us coffee. We sat down for a good late morning chat.

I felt like an early retiree, discharged from my life and work by cancer.

The whole time I was in the garden, I was inhaling the

world, breathing in life, absorbing childhood, gathering strength, and thinking as little as possible. At noon, my dad went to fire up the barbeque and my mom prepared salads and side dishes. We sat together to eat. I felt so ordinary, pleasant and normal in these simple family moments. In this quality time, this calm and un-borrowed time, there is a strength and a steady sanity. In that role of daughter not mother, my shoulders a little less heavy, I managed to raise my head above the water.

January 24, 2018

Half-Full Glasses

What's great about rock bottom is that things can only improve from there.

I'm still not all put together. There are cracks in places, and everything is a little unstable. Moments of laughter and moments of tears merge or meet sharply, trickling through the cracks left by the break that reality glued back together.

The fear is still alive within me.

I can hear it breathing.

I can't seem to neutralize it and, following recent events, it has grown even stronger. With every bodily sensation, it whispers in my ear: I'm spreading.

With every twinge in my neck, every swollen lymph node, every doubt about the new course of treatment

— I am jarred by those dissonant whispers of doubt.

So today I'm countering it by filling half glasses.

I fill the first half glass for the miracle of discovering my cancer early: there is still time to treat it and recover.

I fill the second half glass for discovering the swollen lymph node, thanks to its bizarre but fortuitous reaction to an inflammation that I had. Now we can treat it with radiation. After all, we could easily have been negligent on account of ignorance.

The third half glass is for switching the treatment protocol, thanks to which I'll be able to get the targeted therapy sooner — a new frontier of cancer treatment that is known to be very successful.

I fill the fourth half glass for the fact that I've received half of the truly aggressive substances for the current treatment to really give this tumor a beating from every angle.

I raise these four half glasses in a toast — to life!

To my life!

The first glass is for Autumn — in which I discovered the disease.

The second glass is for Winter — in which I began the drug therapy.

The third glass is for Spring — in which I will undergo

surgery and be cleansed of cancer.

The fourth glass is for Summer — in which I will complete radiation therapy and other complementary treatments to bring me closer to recovery.

And to a healthy and whole self in the coming year!

Amen.

January 29, 2018

Twists and Turns

A few nights ago, as I lay in bed before falling asleep, I remembered our family trip to Italy last summer.

Assaf had prepared a few possible day trips that we could choose from, depending on the weather and what we felt like doing. One evening, we had a family meeting and decided that the next day we would go to a lake that was supposed to be particularly special. The kids' participation in deciding the destination was significant, since it would be an hour and-a-half drive in each direction.

The next morning, we set off. The navigation system decided to take us on an adventure via the old roads that zigzag through the entire mountain range. The roads became increasingly dilapidated and we scarcely saw another car as we continued up and down each mountain.

The drive lasted a very long time and the children began to grow impatient. Yotam felt horribly nauseous, even after we stopped to breathe in the mountain air.

We brought out the "big guns" to get through the rest of the drive (though it was not clear how much longer it would last, because the GPS kept adding time until it did not even remotely resemble the original time estimate): toys, songs, trivia, and limitless Pringles.

My stomach twisted in knots. I was worried we were making a mistake.

The route was stunning, but we knew that as far as we had made it, we would have as much road to cover on the drive back. I felt like this much effort just to see a lake that was still not even visible on the horizon was pushing it. And maybe... maybe we should turn around.

Assaf was optimistic. He said that since we had come this far, we should just push on a little further and make the effort to get there. Somehow, something about his calm soothed my concerns and we kept on driving.

At a certain point, the secluded, mountainous landscape was replaced by that of a small town, which only confused us further. At least we were glad we could tell the kids that we had reached a stop (with or without a lake). The moment the car stopped, the kids and I jumped out like bandits to stretch our legs and blow off some steam.

Now the goal was clear: to find the lake.

I looked everywhere in this tiny two-store town center and decided to follow some people I saw. We had only walked a few paces when I spotted a stand selling all kinds of flotation devices, water shoes and the rest of it — and I was elated. As far as I could tell, this was as good as a sign that said, "Lake!"

A few steps farther I saw a welcoming little lawn with some beach umbrellas. As I got closer, the real treasure was revealed. We suddenly found ourselves before a beautiful azure lake, surrounded by vast, high mountains. Not wind but a breeze of serenity ruffled our hair.

It had all been worth this moment.

Everything that came afterwards only reinforced that feeling. We bathed in the freezing lake water, swam with the fish, rented a paddleboat and pedaled all around the lake. It turned out to be huge, much bigger than what was visible, as it folded around the slope of one of the mountains.

"To the buoy of the dam," Yotam stood on the boat and pointed into the distance.

"Ahoy, Captain!" said Assaf and we pedaled.

Our legs hurt and there was still a long way to pedal back the entire way we had come but we didn't want the moment to end; we weren't finished with the beautiful birds flying by, the cave we saw in the mountains, the spray of freezing water that we made sure to splash in, refreshing our bodies and laughing heartily.

***

When I recalled that experience, a moment before falling asleep, I mainly thought of the similarity between that and the journey that I'm on now. How sometimes my stomach flips from the difficulties my children face with this illness, and how much the navigation to health and recovery is tricky and requires reassessing the route; the ETA gets longer and longer and you can't see the destination. And sometimes the roads are so broken that your whole body hurts from all the bouncing and you wonder to yourself if perhaps you had gone the wrong way. Maybe you should cut your losses and turn around now and go somewhere else, somewhere easier.

But like on the trip, also now, a little piece of heaven on earth awaits me: a healthy life surrounded by everyone I love awaits me. I may not see it yet and maybe it will be a long time until I see that gorgeous lake, surrounded by enormous mountains like roadblocks that will only open to those who are up to the challenge.

We will face that challenge.

Even with the nausea and the body pain, the fear and the worries, with the cracks in the road, with resilience and faith, still — I believe we will get there.

Today I ventured forth on a new path. It will be different and special in its own way, for better and for worse. I will search for my lake, the serenity, and the relaxation in the bosom of my family, among a variety of therapies, between long hours of infusions and strange and different side effects.

Yesterday we got a quick flash of the very edge of the lake; when we got back the ultrasound results, we discovered that the tumor responded well to the treatments and had shrunken impressively.

My first response was relief. Surrounded by the hospital's breast imaging team, we smiled a lot, spreading our happiness. I was upbeat and excited. I hadn't expected anything from these results, certainly not after the supraclavicular lymph node episode.

In the corridor right after we left the exam room, I hugged Assaf in a triumphant embrace.

But then fear came over me again.

I was afraid that maybe it was too early to celebrate. The road is still long and I'm still far from being healthy. I thought it might be better to moderate the 'high' of joy, so as not to fall so low if something goes wrong again.

We went outside into the cold air which cooled down the nonstop thinking engine of my mind and sat on a stone bench that froze our butts but our hearts were aflame with happiness and I told Assaf how strange it was that exactly one week ago I sat on freezing stone crying my eyes out into the earth and to the heavens, and a week later, I'm sitting on a freezing bench feeling happy. It feels like this cancer is a terrifying roller coaster, making you feel your most extreme emotions across the entire spectrum of your soul.

***

As for the way back from the lake, sometimes life holds surprises. We discovered a wonderful route that took us from that extraordinary lake right back to our lovely place in a very short time, quickly and easily.

THIRD
CHEMOTHERAPY
TREATMENT

I've been lying in bed for days thinking how and when will my fingers type again? What will I write? Who will read it? I think of the story of Samson again. This treatment has been my "let me die with the Philistines."

There were moments when I felt it's me or it. Moments when my eyes went dark, my face was covered in cold sweat, and my whole body shook like a drug addict in withdrawal. My hands won't cooperate, my stomach spits out everything I try to give it and there is nothing in the world that can save you from yourself.
And then there's the loneliness.
There's so much loneliness in this struggle. Everyone can help with everything except this feeling. All I want is to breathe without pain, or just to keep breathing.
Me, not it.
During the long days in bed, I thought a lot about life's crazy race for education, a good job, a home,

*family and children, the desire for meaning, to
have an influence.*

*I thought of all the things we accumulate in our
modern lives and the great frustration that in these
lonely moments, none of those things can help me.*

In the end, it's a head-to-head battle.

*It's the most existential battle there is, for basic
independence, for the ability to drink, to go to the
restroom alone, or from the bedroom to the living
room, to eat, to shower, to wrap an arm around
a little boy who just got out of his warm bed and
came to be close to his mommy.*

*It's a battle for the ability to remain cast by the
side of the road and survive while my home life
keeps on going, without me.*

*It's a battle for the ability to hear your children
asking after your presence, both practical and emotional, and not to be able to respond and the guilty
feelings that eat at you from inside all the while.*

It's a quiet, bloodless battle,

Just cold sweat and a pillow soaked with tears.

The Hippopotamus and Crocodile Hunt
by Peter Paul Rubens (1615-1616)

February 14, 2018

Losing My Senses

Two-and-a-half weeks have passed since the last round of chemo and still I'm not myself.

These are my "good" days, yet I feel like something inside me is unfocused. My vision is a little blurry, a little floaty. Every now and then I feel dizzy, sometimes nauseous. I am lethargic and can't differentiate between flavors.

Food still has texture and smell, but just a memory where flavor used to be.

And life, like my sense of taste, has grown dull. Sometimes I don't fully remember that I'm sick, that I have a long way to go to fight the disease and I'm only living from one hour to the next, day by day. Other times, reality pops into my mind and I remember us sitting before the doctor as he tells us the biopsy results.

I hear fragments of the words: "there are tumor cells."

Visual fragments of the doctor's troubled facial expression.

Fragmented thoughts of that moment from which there is no way back.

Sometimes bitter, sometimes sour, I am stuck in a loop of that moment of finding out.

Just like my food, I may still have looks and texture but I have no taste. Ronit doesn't taste like anything at the moment. I feel flat, drained of the energy that is my nature, devoid of smiles and laughter. Only the crying occasionally flickers on, giving me some expression of emotion: a single taste of life compared with the flavor-ful dish I used to be.

***

Yotam's school celebrated Family Day and I didn't have the strength to get up and go. Yotam sprawled beside me on the bed on Friday morning, crying.

"I want you to come. I don't want just one parent!" he said tearfully.

"I understand, sweetie. But even if it were just the flu, I wouldn't be able to make it."

I hugged him, realizing he'll be late for school, but unlike in the past, I no longer cared quite so much.

He laid his head on me and cried intermittently for a whole hour. I teared up beside him. How much longer can I stand this? How much more can I expect him to understand the situation and my absence from his life while I'm still around? What's the point in pretending or hiding? And around the corner, the next treatment awaits, and I don't have the energy for it, I have nothing left to give of myself — but it isn't senseless. It will give me back my life.

February 18, 2018

"It ain't how hard you can hit. It's how hard you can get hit and keep moving forward."

Like the plagues of Egypt, the side effects have really started to hit mercilessly in the past three weeks.

This time my body decided to try out the entire repertoire.

The physical difficulty is also tremendously challenging emotionally. I feel broken, despondent, and introverted. There is much crying and above all, fear. I fear the next round and the treatments after that. I'm afraid of not living up to the challenge.

Surely if today, the day before the next treatment, I don't feel as strong as I did before the previous one, it means I'm starting from an inferior position.

I am a realist. Analytical. A physicist at heart, evidently. I calculate how the side effects will reduce my energy, and it is already low, meaning it will be worse than last time. Initial heights and starting points and potential energy will monstrously transform into functions of side effects and energy attrition.

Still following? Never mind. Bear with me a little. Show some solidarity.

But maybe I'm looking at it all wrong. Maybe if we stick with Newton's physics, we will find that actually from a lower starting point, there's less distance to fall, at a lower speed, so maybe there will be less shock to the system? Maybe it actually won't be as bad as the last time? Maybe the blow won't hurt as much?

I had no real respite. I had wanted to give myself the kind of break that lets the lungs fill up with cancer-free oxygen to help fight, cope, survive the difficulties and triumph.

But I have been blessed with these insightful guys in my life, both adults and children, who are able to give me the strength, the focus, and the words I need to hear. They help me lift myself up to a healthy level of mental resilience, the day before the treatment so I can assure myself that I will survive the next horror to come.

Assaf, whose roots are strong and steady, embraced

and caressed me and wiped away my tears as he helped me to focus on two main points:

The first, harsh reality: I have no choice.

To illustrate the second point, he brought me back, as if in a time machine, to the first meeting with my oncologist. At the beginning of the conversation, she asked me what I know at this point. I knew that she was referring to medical details concerning the type of tumor, that sort of thing, but it was actually there with her that the following sentence instinctively escaped my lips: "I know that I want to live."

"So has anything changed since then?" Assaf asked me.

"No," I answered him, mainly to myself, reiterating this will of mine, which, amidst the dehydrating hallucinations, pain, weakness, diarrhea, vomiting and hot flashes, may have been forgotten. With eyes either as dry as the desert or crying nonstop like a rainstorm, the goal became as blurry as everything else.

My father and mentor, who has always been a listening ear for me and a source of encouragement in hard times, added this additional bit of insight: "People do great things thanks to their spirit, not their strength."

"You have good friends, a loving family, a supportive

husband and children that give you a reason to get up in the morning even when things are hard," he said.

I breathed in his words.

My enchanting children, Yotam and Saar, the little guys in my life, have granted me support in their special way, in their actions rather than their words. One evening, as we were doing the regular nighttime preparations, I was feeling so ill that Assaf came to be with me in the bedroom. My whole body was shaking out of control, and in the meantime the boys were running wild in the living room.

I felt uneasy that I was robbing them of him when they needed his assistance in getting organized. With admirable calm, split between two kids and one geriatric lady, he said that they could wait and nothing bad would happen. I let myself take a break from managing, commanding, being the one in control (of everything aside from my own trembling body), and I snuggled against him.

When Yotam came into the bedroom, I took advantage of the opportunity to tell him that I was feeling really bad, that Dad was helping me at the moment, and I would like it if they could start getting themselves ready for bed.

The moment the bedroom door closed, the two boys joined forces under Yotam's command. He took Saar, got him showered and dressed, brushed his teeth, put him in bed and read him a bedtime story while getting himself ready, too. He gave me the gift of his father for half-an-hour, to be my partner alone and comfort me in my moment of crisis.

Their support just then moved me deeply and showed me again how much everyone, the little ones to the adults was getting on board for my sake, so I would have to summon my inner strength for them, too.

There is no better way to begin the race than with the quote from Rocky Balboa: "Nobody is gonna hit as hard as life, but it ain't how hard you can hit. It's how hard you can get hit and keep moving forward. It's how much you can take and keep moving forward. That's how winning is done."

FOURTH
CHEMOTHERAPY
TREATMENT

In this war of mine there are no sides
Who is animal and who human?
Who is the destroyer and who the savior?
A blend of heavens and earth
Spirit and matter
Living and dead
Elevated or cast down
White hope
Against a black background.

In this war of mine
My roots cling to the ground
My branch broken by the ferocity of battle
In my war
I am left naked of leaves
Of myself
And of who I once was.

In this war of mine
I will be forced to adapt
To yellowing leaves
And amputated branches
Surrounded by human scars
From the wounds of battle
And from my remaining earthbound roots
I will sprout myself anew.

War, 1984 by Henri Rousseau

March 7, 2018

In Sickness and in Health...

When Sunday morning began, I could not have imagined how fast it would deteriorate.

Assaf, who in the last two months seems to have developed exceptional foresight, felt it coming and stayed by my side.

At 9 AM I was still saying, "Overall, I feel fine."

By 10 AM, I felt my power draining from me and I had to lie down in bed. An hour later we were on our way to the hospital.

When we arrived, I was leaning on him, barely able to stand up.

Even though I was quickly admitted, every minute felt like an eternity until I was laying down in a bed, hooked up to an IV.

The blood tests showed major deficiencies of important bodily resources, which I had lost on account of my stomach's new tendency to eject anything and everything that entered. Nor was it picky about the direction of exit. The main thing was to void its contents as fast as possible.

After the doctor's examination, it was decided that I should spend the night in the hospital. I panicked.

Apart from when I'd given birth, which is a healthy event, I had never spent the night in a hospital before.

I didn't want to be far from home, the kids, my bed, and even my bathroom. But the staff insisted. They stressed that I might collapse at home unexpectedly. I gave in.

So, I got to have the inpatient experience: wheelchair transport from one test to another, and food that made me feel like I was in a nursing home just by looking at it. (Who else eats jello?)

But the team on the ward was wonderful. Only now, having seen them up close, do I fully appreciate how hard the work of the dedicated doctors and nurses is, and how important it is to properly reward these people who workday and night for patients' well-being, with a smile and pleasant concern.

***

As the evening wore on, and it got late, and I suggested Assaf go home.

I wanted him to eat, rest, and recuperate. It had been a long, difficult day for him, too.

But he didn't want to go and leave me there alone.

Suddenly, I realized that ever since Saar was born, three-and-a-half years ago, I hadn't spent a night alone outside of the house. Of course, that was a choice.

I'm aware that it's hard for me to leave them.

Even when suggestions arose of going away with a girlfriend for a weekend, I always felt uncomfortable leaving unless it was truly necessary.

I thought it would feel sad for them: a weekend without their mother.

These days, even when I'm in the house, there are times when I feel so unwell that they are forced to go out without me or even manage at home without my involvement while I lie in bed, not myself, staying close to the bathroom.

And each time, being separated from them makes me terribly sad. Something inside me seeks that family wholeness, which is achieved only when all of us are together.

After an hour, I asked Assaf again to go for a bit to give himself a break. I assured him that the staff was taking good care of me and that I was fine, hooked up to the infusion. Everything was under control.

He went as far as the door, then came back.

He put on his coat, went and came back.

It was as though he were departing from me in baby steps, each time increasing the distance, and every step from him accompanied by a tear from me. Not just because it was hard for me, but because I saw how hard it was for him.

Finally, we managed to part. After he left my sight, a gust of loneliness entered the room. I cried a little and then recalled my time in the maternity ward. It was a Friday night, far from the family (which, at the time, was Assaf and Yotam) when I decided to go and take the new member of the family, who was waiting for me in the nursery. I have the image etched in my mind: me coming back to the room with him, sitting down in the armchair and cradling him in my arms while the lonely discomfort disappeared to go find its next victim.

This time, the feeling passed pretty quickly thanks to conversations with girlfriends and a night visit from Shirley, my best friend, who always knows how to make me happy.

Over the past few weeks, I have become well-practiced with visiting the hospital for infusions, unable to overcome the rate of my fluid loss. One time, Shirley came to pick me up from home to go for an IV infusion. I was sitting powerless in the kitchen while Assaf organized everything around me before we left. With every movement of his, I felt the weight of my wretchedness grow, like the burden that I am on everybody. Then the door opened, and Shirley entered like a ray of sunshine.

"Heeeeey!" she called out with an unparalleled grace, spread her hands wide as she came towards me. The moment I saw her walking toward me, I burst into tears.

"What happened?" she asked, pulling me into her big hug, so I wouldn't fall or fall apart.

I didn't know what had happened. There was no particular incident but just seeing her coming toward me and bringing such great happiness with her into my deep sadness like a tsunami, flooded me with feelings.

Now, again, she brought me happiness and support, and the night passed without sadness.

To my delight, Assaf also had a surprise waiting for him at home in the form of a friend with a hamburger and beer who had come to cheer him up.

Each time anew, I am grateful for the special friends surrounding us, in good times and bad, in sickness and in health. Within their own hectic, daily lives, they find ways to give us little moments of happiness throughout this difficult journey that our family is on.

FIFTH
CHEMOTHERAPY
TREATMENT

You who stands there
Raising your arm between fights
Between the previous round's days of victory
In which you tasted just a sample of life
And the days of pain and breaking
Of the present struggle
In which your body is bereft of everything you are
And all the strength you had
You just want the darkness to be finished
The light to rise and with it you will raise your arm
Victorious
In another fight against IT:
Against yourself
Against your body
Against your strengths
Against the power of spirit
To rise up from the earth
Toward the air
To scorch the fire
And cross the water.

You who stands there
Your face stoic and ready
And your arm raised above
Between the fights
Give me strength
To raise mine.

Mademoiselle V... in the Costume of an Espada,
by Edouard Manet, 1862

March 18, 2018

What Goes In —
Will Soon Come Out

Meals during the period of chemotherapy were a two-way street. Almost every meal that I ate had to be tasted again on its way out. So, in addition to the medical and nutritional considerations — a diet rich in magnesium and potassium and a LOT of water — like sailors on a ship, I got to know the backward taste of food and to consider what I wanted to eat according to what was less terrible to throw up.

Assaf told me that sailors in the navy, experienced at tasting their food on its way out, had decided that ice cream was best. I tried that, too. I wasn't particularly impressed, but it was less horrible than other things.

Let's call a spade a spade. The worst side effects of

chemo, apart from the weakness, are the vomiting and diarrhea, which only make you weaker. The nausea makes it hard to be near food, even when it's possible to eat. I try to sit with Assaf and the kids while they're eating and drink a glass of water or tea. Other times, I go sit in the living room so that I'm still nearby, but the scent of food won't reach my nose. Saar, who doesn't understand what's going on, has tried to force feed me a number of times.

"Mommy have some schnitzel," he offers with his little hand.

"No, thank you sweetheart," I answer him politely.

"Take it," he insists. "It's good for you," and tries to push it into my mouth.

I move his hand as gently as I possibly can with my mounting nausea.

"I promise that I'll eat later, after my nausea passes," I tell him, hoping he understands and isn't offended.

The nausea turns over whatever's left in my stomach, while at the same time, my heart is filled with this moment's sweet laughter.

April 9, 2018

The Monster is Coming

I knew it was about to come.

Experience had taught me how it is supposed to look, sound and feel.

Even its timing should be predictable at this point.

And yet the expectation of the monster, knowing that it would be coming soon but not knowing exactly when, and the tension and fatigue of searching for it in every rustling sound, in every sensation — it takes over. It's like a missile coming at me but I don't know when it will get here, from which direction or at what speed, and my neck hurts from scanning the sky and my eyes are tired of following it... That's what it's like with the monster. I find myself ambushed in bed in a dark room, covered up to my chin with a blanket. Waiting for it.

In the darkness of these thoughts, I understood what FDR meant when he said that "the only thing we have to fear... is fear itself." That eased me out of the ambush. I cannot permit myself to fear the fear. The war is being waged in my body yet also in my head, in my thoughts, in striving to hold my head up even in my lowest moments.

At this stage of chemo, when I already feel well-versed in the treatments and the side effects and can draw up tables and calculate statistics about when each round of side effects should turn up, I wonder if it's a strength that enables me to prepare, or a weakness that feeds the monsters in the dark?

Finally, the monster arrived, several hours after the moment that I decided not to stop, not to fear the fear.

It came, I looked it in the eyes and told it:

"Welcome — I've been waiting for you. Together you and I will defeat this cancer."

SIXTH
CHEMOTHERAPY
TREATMENT

*I wish to speed up time, get there already, free
from chemo, hopefully for good.
To return to rocking gently like most people, not a
tsunami every three weeks.
I begin to hear the calm, the melody of the waves
and the unfolding of victory flags above me.
I just begin to see the calm, like the sea peeking
through the buildings at the end of Tel Aviv streets.
I am beginning to feel the calm, a mesmerizing
azure, dotted with sailboats like envoys of freedom
that move to and fro to the far reaches of my soul.
I begin to breathe the calm, the sea breeze
caressing us at the balcony's edge,
Guiding my white sails to safer shores.
The calm is here, almost close enough to touch.*

*There remain journeys ahead, like the tangled
greenery on the porch railings, separating me from
the caress of the water, from the outside world,
from what I have gone through and what my
future holds.
This moment, this moment in which I am
immersed in this elixir of calm,
Only it exists.
The calm and me.*

Garden at Sainte-Adresse by Claude Monet, 1867

April 3, 2018

No Escape

For a long while after I was diagnosed, I couldn't concentrate on anything. In the evenings, Assaf would turn on the television but I would just stare into space. Nothing interested me and I was unable to escape my reality, even for a moment. I couldn't read books or watch TV. I would lie there for hours at a time, unable to move, wallowing in my thoughts, unable to disconnect. The next stage was to read inspirational books about overcoming illness. A friend of ours sent me Lance Armstrong's book about coping with cancer. Shirley, my best friend, bought me yet another book. I managed to read a few chapters of each. That was a major achievement.

One of my sisters-in-law tried to convince me to find a TV series that would engage my imagination, take my mind off things. It was two months before I got to the point of being able to enjoy a show and practice the art of escapism.

A few weeks later I started to read a regular prose book and to my surprise, I finished it. After that I read another and the ability to focus on things that weren't cancer improved. It was always, however, for short amounts of time, and only on my 'good' days, not so much on my bad days.

The thing was that even when I managed to escape cancer, I discovered that the universe had not forgotten and that it was everywhere.

In the first series I watched, an Australian program about the years following World War Two, a totally marginal character was diagnosed with breast cancer and forced to undergo radical surgery (which was common practice in those days). In the show, they portray her fear of her hot-tempered husband, lest he be angry with her because now she is defective, mutilated.

I switched to a comedy. There, I told myself, cancer wouldn't find me. But I was wrong. The heroine's mother is found to have breast cancer and she deliberates between preventative mastectomy of both breasts versus the removal of just one. Furthermore, they show her stubbornness not to lose her hair at the cost of sitting with a helmet of ice on her head throughout the hours of chemo, shaking and suffering until she breaks down and takes the helmet off. In one of the treatments she discovers that her chemo-buddy who had sat beside her, died unexpectedly because of the disease's rapid deterioration. Everything in the name of drama. But this was supposed to be a comedy! I told myself.

Even in the four books I read, there were three breast cancer patients and one with lung cancer. How could that be? After all, these were books on topics that weren't even related to cancer.

Recently, I decided to read a fifth book. On page 23, a breast tumor is discovered, and I abandoned it.

It feels like enough already. Enough of this disease being endlessly used for the sake of drama. I realize that it's common and that it gives a shock to the plot, suspense for the reader and even empathy for the character, but as someone going through it, I feel that it's abusive to those of us among the audience.

Maybe someone should mark these books like they mark the packaging of products that weren't tested on animals.

Let us escape.

For now, I feel like any attempt at escape, brings me right back to where I started.

April 14, 2018

Memories and Remembrances

When I made the appointment, I didn't notice that it was set for Israel's Holocaust Remembrance Day[2].

Chemotherapy, with its array of side effects, does not distinguish between day and night, the work week or the weekend, and certainly does not attach any significance to holidays. As a result, my calendar is full of treatment dates and follow-up appointments, which do not necessarily take such events into consideration.

The siren caught me in the lobby of the treatment center. A minute-long siren sounds on the morning of this day, each year, to commemorate those who perished in the Holocaust. As I stood there with my head bowed,

---

2   This takes place on a different date than the annual international Holocaust Remembrance Day

the siren blasting through the internal speaker in the low ceiling, I noticed all the patients standing in silence. I was deeply moved.

Here is a group of people who have not been terribly fortunate lately, struggling for their lives, and they are standing for the siren. Some of them lean on canes, some lean against the wall, using the life force that they still have to honor those who did not make it out alive.

From that stronghold of the unwell, moving between life and death, I felt lucky to be able to honor the memory and heroism of those who perished. In this world where we are so accustomed to planning ahead, having control and securing ourselves from every possible angle, the last few months have taught me to live precisely the opposite way, from one hour to the next, because nothing is predictable nor self-evident.

No, nothing can be taken for granted: not simple functions like getting out of bed, walking to the living room, showering, eating, digesting, and certainly not planning activities outside the house. But more than anything, I have no idea who I will be when I come out the other side of this labyrinth.

What kind of life will I want for myself? What insights will guide me? Will I be constantly looking over my shoulder to check if cancer is still chasing me?

I am learning to live differently.

I am touched by the small things, like when I am able to cook something for my family and watch the kids gorge on the forgotten food that Mommy makes — their mother who for months now has not been functioning as they know and remember.

In powerless moments, an image arises from just a year ago, of me stopping on the way to a writing class at my regular coffee shop in Tel Aviv and buying a cheese stick. I walk along and my face is caressed by the sea breeze.

That memory of freedom and air, calm and tranquility, is my lighthouse.

I also remember the moments when I allowed life to disturb that serenity. I remember phone calls from work that interrupted my sense of calm, making me forget to feel the air, see the waterfront, or taste the cheese stick. I just sat restlessly and waited for the class to end — this class that I had been waiting for all week — so I could take care of this work thing that demanded my attention.

I want to grow and not let the pressures of life dictate my enjoyment. Not to let moments of anger take over. Not to take things too much to heart. I now have an intimate knowledge of how detrimental that is to one's health.

I hope that I will be able to be better to myself, more forgiving, more relaxed, less judgmental. I hope that I will know to let go of the quest for perfection and the frustration of not achieving it. I hope that I will choose the next steps well and understand what does and does not really matter at every crossroad.

***

On the last national Memorial Day, which takes place each year one week after Holocaust Remembrance Day, I attended the ceremony with Yotam. He was seven years old then and it was the first time we had exposed him to the sadness of life.

We sat silently together, listening to the heartbreaking texts being read aloud, of a father who did not return, of a brother, a sister, a daughter, a son.

The silence outside did not reflect the storm in my heart.

During a piece about a mother killed in a suicide bomb attack, who never returned to the bosom of her family, I felt Yotam's arms wrap around me and his head rest on my body, as if to shield him from the pain.

I held him to me, kissing his head and petting him, removing some of the sadness that had landed on him like leaves blown by a stormy wind.

Who would have believed that within less than a year, our lives would be shaken too? Who would have thought that suddenly my own presence in the lives of my sons would not be so self-evident?

A few days from now that annual Memorial Day will return, just a few days before the next treatment. I am deliberating whether or not to attend the ceremony again, this time with my eye-catching cancer-patient look.

I pray that the day will come when this period of time will be just a distant memory, to be remembered and not forgotten.

SEVENTH
CHEMOTHERAPY
TREATMENT

To charge
With full force
Even when there's none left.
Be the warlord,
The warrior,
The spear.
Be all of it
In order to be.

To charge
Again and again
Each battle anew.
Don't rest, do not take root in the ground,
Be one with the body,
Be present in the heart.
Be all of it
In order to be.

To charge
With the colors of fire and earth
In the scarlet hues,
White touches of purity
With no surrender,

No truce —
Be whole,
Be strong,
Be all of it
In order to be.

Battle by Eugene Delacroix 1798-1863

May 2, 2018

Superheroes

It's my first evening out of bed in a week, socializing with the residents of the house, reminding them how I look when I'm upright. Sitting upright, that is, because standing up still makes me dizzy. It's a new dimension for me and a small sign of success each time.

Toward midnight, Saar came out of his room and asked for water. I was just on my way to the bedroom when I stopped to look at this rosy cherub, dressed in his Spiderman pajamas and ready to vanquish all the evil in the world.

While Assaf went to bring him water, I tried to be a superhero myself, and I decided to lift him up and take him back to bed. Despite being very sleepy, he smiled happily as he realized I was going to pick him up and hugged me back for all four steps to his bed.

Afterward, as I lay in my bed trying to fall asleep, I thought about how this all must look from his perspective. Maybe it seemed like a dream in which Mommy was better and not sick anymore? Mommy who lovingly lifts him to her and doesn't just reach out a weak hand from her sick bed to stroke him. Mommy who can take him to or from nursery school, can give him his bath and pick him up whenever he wants, and a mom who can join in the holiday celebrations at nursery school. Perhaps at these moments in his dream he is already seeing our new path through life, where I am totally healthy and entirely theirs.

Will he remember this tomorrow morning? Will it make him happy or sad?

I want my little Spiderman to think that he can save the good and triumph over bad, at least for a few more innocent years. So, in the face of the remaining chemo and the many hardships that it heaps upon me, I have to be a superhero, too.

I must be a heroine for the upcoming surgery, to overcome the fear, pain and uncertainty, the radiation which follows and the fearful shadow of cancer even afterwards.

After all, I was a superhero to a tiny boy in his

Spiderman pajamas, who got carried, hugged, and kissed at midnight from a strong mother who previously was unable even to carry herself.

EIGHTH
CHEMOTHERAPY
TREATMENT

I don't want marathons, or wars, I want to embrace life, every moment of it, and linger on. I want to collect these moments of beauty, and to pile them upon one another, like a pillar of light made of joy, lovingly radiating back at everyone around me.

Work/Piece/Display by Dani Ossia
Petrushka Square - Beilinson Hospital
Photograph courtesy of Rabin Medical Center

May 21, 2018

On Edge

I know the path that awaits me. I've walked it before, over and over, all those previous times. It was always hard on the body and the mind. And now, just a few steps from the finish line — it is more burdensome than ever.

I know not to expect the promised land beyond them, not yet. It's the end of an exhausting chapter that is hard to put into words, no matter how much I've tried.

I know that the days will pass, and this stretch of path will pass with them. But this stretching on and on, like a wad of chewing gum, is straining my nerves, as wrecked as they already are. At the beginning, when they told me "chemotherapy, "I said — "Bring it on, I've got endurance, I'm not afraid of pain."

What I hadn't considered was the patience it takes to manage for such a long, ongoing period of illness. It's not tolerance one needs here — that's a novice mistake — you need perseverance, determination and forgiveness towards yourself for the days when you didn't fight your best. You need patience, a lot of patience, acceptance and understanding that this is your life right now — a big black hole of side effects, a soup of uncertainty.

But I learned that the hard way, cried more than a little and learned a great deal, about myself and those around me. It has been the hardest lesson in my entire life's history and, moreover, the lesson most carved into my bones. I learned the importance of a supportive environment that weaves a flexible safety net, one that can wrap around you securely, but also bounce back and stabilize to make the next leap.

I am supposed to finish chemo at the end of the month.

My life has been on hold for 150 days.

One hundred and fifty days in which Assaf, besides fathering the two little ones, has been taking care of me, henceforth "nursing" me, while demonstrating a remarkable ability to overcome his fear of needles.

One hundred and fifty days in which he has looked after me day and night, while simultaneously working, managing the home and the children's social life.

One hundred and fifty days in which he takes me to doctors for checkups and infusions and buys medicines at a frequency that has entitled him to personal calls from the head pharmacist.

One hundred and fifty days in which my parents are on the lookout, sleeping with one eye open, waiting for a sudden wake-up call, experiencing my chemo from the sidelines.

One hundred and fifty days of powerful and supportive friendships, of a community that helps and holds us, of encouragement from coworkers.

One hundred and fifty days of family — the one I was born into, and the one that was created around me.

One hundred and fifty days in which my children live through their mother's journey to recovery, always hugging, cheering, and showing quiet understanding: restraint that is not at all characteristic of their age.

To honor all of that, I choose to remove my headscarf today. I march these last few steps thanks to each and every one of the people who have supported me, but mostly for my little nestlings.

Soon I will cross the finish line, with my hands raised in triumph, and each of my children holding one of my legs, like pillars of my strength.

June 7, 2018

The Day After

I have waited so long for this moment! The hardship is behind me, my strength is slowly returning (although slower than I had expected) and my mood has improved. I am more myself than I have been in the entire half-year that's just passed.

The joy that I feel is so enormous and overwhelming, that I could almost get confused and think I've already recovered.

And maybe that wouldn't be a mistake.

Maybe there really is no secret agent remaining inside me.

And even if some of its cells remain, maybe my thinking that I've recovered would be the final blow to eliminate them? As if through absolute denial of their existence, I'll achieve a state where my thoughts manifest reality?

Two weeks from now I will undergo the operation. That will leave me in another physical hiatus for several weeks, so these days until that surgery are extra precious to me. Each and every hug becomes special. I take them in, trying to store them up for the days when hugging will be a challenge because moving my arm will be painful.

I celebrated my birthday under the shadow of chemo. The side effects of the last round were particularly intense, but to my delight, I already felt significantly better a few days later. This year I received a lot of love, more attention than usual. My surroundings must have sensed the need to compensate me for this year and my loss of self.

I was only frustrated by the feeling that time had been stolen from me, as though someone had reached a hand into my life and took away six months soon to become a full year. I want to claim my previous age back. I didn't feel like I was living during that time, so how can it count? And how can I be expected to celebrate a year in which only six months of it was living and the other half was a protracted, painful attempt to survive?

Time has taken on special meaning now, a contradictory meaning.

On the one hand, I want to take things slowly, calmly, not race against the clock. On the other hand, I want to take advantage and enjoy every moment, because none of us knows how much time we have left on the planet.

When it's quiet in the house, I hear the recovering cells in my body telling me, "Stop, stop!"

"Stop what?" I ask them. "After all, there is so much to be done. Organize things around the house? Little projects that were neglected during the chemo? Take care of the never-ending bureaucracy and form-filling of the health system? I want to go out and have fun, to meet friends, go wild with the kids, swallow life whole!"

"What's more important to you?" I ask myself because it's really hard for me to decide. Everything seems important, and I simply can't achieve it all.

"What will make you happy?" They respond immediately. "Because whatever makes you happy makes us stronger. And whatever exhausts you weakens us."

And then I understand how intelligent my body cells are. Maybe because, unlike me, they had to live alongside those cancerous cells that threatened to annihilate them, even before I knew I was sick. They have the perspective and insights from within a world of survival.

Dealing with the infinite projects that have accumulated and clearly must be attended to with some degree of urgency is akin to running in a hamster wheel, only without the fun. You always come back to the same point. It never feels like you've made progress.

I choose to listen to my cells and build the path to my own happiness, to health, to sanity and to an active place in my family.

IN BETWEEN

I look back on the way I've come
And that which remains before me.
I want to tip the scales,
To see with my own eyes that most of it is behind me,
To appreciate the weight of the suffering
That still awaits,
The strength I must summon
In order to survive the rest.
How many more pearls of thought
Will I polish with my pain?
How many more insights can I find in their clear
reflection,
Like a crystal ball?
Beaded necklaces of treatments and pains
Hold a glimmer of hope
To shine for days,
Envelop life,
Feel the pulse
Of my heartbeat.

Woman Holding a Balance
by Johannes Vermeer, 1662-1663

June 19, 2018

One in Seven

One in seven? One in eight? It's not one in nine anymore.

This period between chemo and surgery has outed me into public life. Feeling better, I have allowed myself more than just a short walk around the neighborhood, and plan a date night at a sold-out show in a theater that seats seven hundred. I was singled out, the only one who stood out as "the ill one" – the one with the headscarf, the bald one, the one with the invisible writing across her forehead that says: 'I have cancer'. One in seven hundred.

Last weekend we went to a seaside resort to spend some quality family time together. Even there I felt burned. Not by the salty seawater or the jellyfish but by the looks I received.

It's not that I'm blaming anyone. It's alright to look. But those glances just emphasized my sense of difference. In a hotel of about seven hundred people, I was the only one who stood out as "the ill one" – the one with the headscarf, the bald one, the one with the invisible writing across her forehead that says 'I have cancer'.

The glances in the dining room, pitying looks at the poor cancer-inflicted woman with two little kids, looks at the pool at the woman wrapped from head to toe in sun protective clothing. Each time I encountered such a glance, something inside me shrank.

I felt shame, sadness, and anger, too.

That weekend I was, once again, one of seven hundred.

At the hospital, you get the feeling that everyone's sick, that it's very common, that there is no real reason to feel like you were specifically selected to 'get screwed' or drew the wrong lottery ticket. But when you zoom out you discover that despite the prevalence of the disease, most people are healthy.

The sadness that this revelation brought me was replaced by anger at this twisted bingo that I had won. I'm angry for what my family and I had to go through, angry about the surgery that is scheduled for thirty-six hours from now and frightens me terribly, angry about the destruction the chemo left me with, angry about the devastation that will remain after the surgery, and angry at the desolation that the future radiation will bring. I am embittered that from now on, I must stay alert and look over my shoulder all the time, more than anybody who has not been touched by cancer.

During takeoff on the flight back, it sounded like the engine was slowing down. My heart jumped in my chest and I thought what a shame it would be to die like that, after I had suffered for half-a-year to survive. What a waste.

As you may have guessed, the flight went fine.

I thought how statistically, the plane is the safest existing mode of transport, but if you should happen to be among those who drew the wrong lottery ticket and got on a plane that crashed — the statistics are irrelevant.

In that moment I realized that whether I am one in seven or one of seven hundred, ever since I was diagnosed, I am one in one. The one who got sick and one that will recover!

SURGERY

On the isle of my uncertainty
Am I the lion
Or the cheetah,
The attacker or the attacked
In the midst of the world's beauty
And a life bright with color
The sun radiant as ever
A lion bites me.
I grasp the grass,
The lion holds me tight,
Paralyzed by pain and fear,
The last of life pulsing through me,

He and I become one
Jumbled mess of hair and baldness.
And on this day
I will close my eyes
As we are separated by the scalpel
By brush,
And I'll awake
A lion.

The Repast of the Lion, 1907, by Henri Rousseau

June 28, 2018

Unilateral Disengagement

At this very hour, precisely one week ago to the day, I separated from my cancer.

I don't know if it willingly agreed to leave my body, and maybe there is no such thing as complete certainty, but I declared unilateral disengagement for the sake of wholeness in my life and that of my family.

When I expressed my fear of surgery to someone who had herself been sick and recovered, she said to me that apart from the relief she felt after the operation had gone well, there is another kind of relief that doesn't get discussed: that the undercover agent that had been with us this whole time, day and night, is gone.

The day after my surgery, I understood what she'd meant about the relief of disengagement. May we never,

ever meet again.

The day before surgery and even the morning of that special day, I was extremely, perhaps bizarrely cheerful. My worry became excitement, and I had the sense of a special event. I spent the morning joking and laughing, accompanied by the best team you could ask for.

Dressed in the characteristic open-backed hospital gown and lying on a bed, I was led to my rebirth. As I waited in the surgery prep room, they began to hook me up to gadgets such as massage socks (I'd recommend them for anyone who wants to feel pampered), and I even received a compliment from the nurse who came over to fill out a form for me and told me how beautiful I was. I don't know if she makes a habit of empowering women who find themselves in one of the least feminine and most embarrassing moments of their lives or if she really admired my appearance, but it was a warm, pleasant feeling, like a massage for my heart. I'm grateful to that kind nurse whose name I don't know.

The entrance to the OR was like the offramp on the highway. There were a ton of people there. Each one introduced himself briefly when it came time to do their part but I didn't catch a thing apart from the great bustle around me. One person grabbed an arm to find a vein (finding a vein on me, particularly after the chemo, was a task that could take much longer than the surgery itself), the next began to mark up my arm with a marker, another connected electrodes to me, and the anesthetist told me that when he put me under he would say 'goodnight' and then I would sleep.

Suddenly, it was as though the cold, bright light of the operating room was freezing the walls of humor that had protected me all these days and hours, and fear began to creep in, hand-in-hand with reality. I panicked. Tears began to flow. My surgeon immediately noticed that I was panicking and came over, placed her hand on my cheek and asked me what was going on. I told her that until now I had been feeling cheerful, but now I was afraid. She smiled and said that if I wasn't afraid she would think something was amiss. At the same time, she gestured to the anesthetist to put me under right away. As I looked at her calming smile, I heard the anesthetist say "Goodnight," and nothing more.

As I write these things, I am moved all over again. For the first time since the surgery, the tears that are falling aren't tears of fear. I wish that all doctors understood how significant their humanity is to the patient, to say nothing of their professionalism and experience. People are driven by emotion and when we are sick it is extra important for us to feel secure as we are led, sometimes without any control, to a safe shore.

***

The following day, a Friday, Assaf sat beside me and we talked about the hours we had spent apart.

"This is the disadvantage of surgery on a Thursday," I told him sadly. "It's a shame that my doctors aren't here over the weekend, just whoever's on call."

"It's not so bad," he assured me. "I am sure that if there's something that the 'on call' doctor needs to update or consult your doctors about, he'll call them."

A few minutes later, my surgeon, accompanied by another surgeon who had been present at the lymph node surgery on my neck, came through the curtain. It took me a few moments to understand what I was seeing. Dressed in everyday clothes and sunglasses, for a moment I didn't recognize them.

"How are you feeling?" she asked me, removing her sunglasses, and smiling broadly.

"Right now, great," I replied. "You won't believe this, but just a few moments ago I told Assaf that it was a shame that my doctors aren't here on the weekends."

"Well, here we are," she said for both of them.

They each checked me.

"I have no feeling in my armpit," I told my surgeon. "Is that normal?"

"Definitely," she laughed with irresistible grace.

"When you put on deodorant, you'll feel that one part has sensation and the other doesn't. That's normal and part of it will return with time." We laughed together. I was relieved just by her presence, scattering light and a sense of security.

"Have you been to the bakery downstairs yet?" she asked Assaf.

"They won't let her get out of bed even though she's been asking to get up since 6 AM," he explained.

"I'll fix that," she said and gave us further instructions.

"When she gets out of bed, take her to the bakery in a wheelchair before they close. Sit there and have some coffee and cake."

She went to speak with the staff and returned and said, "soon they'll come get you out of bed," she smiled. "And you'll go to the bakery, alright? They close at 12 PM. You still have an hour."

"Thanks so much for coming," I said to both of them. "You made my day."

I didn't expect that surprise. There aren't a lot of words to describe how much happiness and relief that visit injected into my day. No substance they had given me intravenously had calmed me like that. Comfort from the heart is the best medicine for recovery.

***

This surgery was my rebirth as a healthy person. Even though the pathologist's results have not come back yet and even though there remains another period of recovery and radiation treatments, I feel different already. Something in my gut is telling me that this is the turning point that will bring me back my life after this long road I've been on.

I probably felt it subconsciously from the moment of diagnosis. Three days after I got the biopsy results, on December 23rd, 2017, I began my first blog, where I wrote: "With the end of Hanukkah and the triumph of light over darkness, I, too, will be like the Earth, and on the day when darkness overcomes light, I will grow and hold the light inside me, each day a little more. And maybe by June 21, the longest day of the year, I can declare my victory of this battle, perhaps even the war."

A week before the operation, after bringing my father to a meeting with his oncologist, we were on our way back from the hospital and it rained. I was amazed that it was raining in the middle of June. It occurred to me that we were nearing the longest day of the year and the official beginning of summer. I suddenly remembered my first blog post, where I had written that hopefully, come the summer solstice, and longest day of the year – I will able to declare my victory of this battle, or even this war. Unbelievably, this is the date set for my surgery.

July 11, 2018

Cracks in my Smile

Ever since leaving the operating room, a smile has not left my face.

But lately, this picture of happiness and relief of being post-surgery, has a few burnt-out pixels.

The drain (whoever doesn't know what that is, I pray that you never have to find out), which at first only startled me, since I'm not used to having a tube coming out of my body, irritates me with almost every movement. I am counting down the days until I'm rid of it. I still can't lift my arm above ninety degrees, so I can only wear button-up shirts and they have to be big and loose to comfortably contain the drain. So, if until now I had enjoyed being looked at on account of my headscarf/ hat/bald head, now I am completing the look with a big man's button-up shirt, which eliminates any hint of femininity. But I must say that the shirt pocket, usually on the left side, is actually very useful.

There are days when I wonder which is the more compelling reason for staying inside: the harsh sun that could do me harm, or the embarrassment of the masculine appearance that is my destiny for these next few weeks.

My hair isn't growing as fast as I would like it to, and I miss it. I miss my feminine appearance and even more than that, I miss my healthy appearance. The headscarves and hats are still my dear friends. I had thought that by this point I would already be 'painting the town red' with a cool Sinead O'Connor hairstyle, like I was just having a little early mid-life crisis. Like I wasn't a person who had been broken and put back together again.

In these little moments, I ask myself since when am I bothered by these trite matters, and maybe it's actually good news that I'm already concerned with appearance rather than survival. Maybe that's what improvement looks like after being in the deepest abyss of my life. Or maybe I'm simply afraid of the pathology result that I'm expecting any day now. Maybe I so desperately want to find out that all the samples came back cancer-free and I'm afraid of any other possible outcome.

Every kind of cancer is hard, but breast cancer is like the universe kicking you in the gut. It's a hard blow to your femininity, taking an organ that is symbolic of feminine beauty and turning it into a double agent or an enemy. The patient is left with cuts, scars and burns, damaged body image, and fear of exposing the wounded body naked. For those in a relationship it is hard to preserve, and for those who are not, it is hard to find. Breastfeeding is no longer a choice.. Each of these is a loss.

Yesterday, Yotam was lying beside me and it felt like he had read my thoughts when he said:

"How funny would it be if you suddenly appeared with head full of hair."

Both of us laughed and then I grew serious.

"Actually, I really miss my hair," I decided to share with him.

"How come?" he asked, and I was surprised by his response. Naively, I had thought it was obvious that I would miss my hair although I often made jokes with them about it.

"Because I look prettier with hair," I answered simply and honestly.

"The headscarf looks good on you, too," he said, surprising me.

"Thank you, my darling boy," I told him. "That makes me feel better and stronger to hear you say that."

I hugged him and for a moment I felt a little more like myself and a little less like a "dude" with my bald head and buttoned shirt.

If only in the next few days, still dressed in my "ninety degree mobility" fashion, I will get good news, news of victory, that in one moment will revive all those burned pixels to my picture of happiness. Amen.

July 24, 2018

Everything You Need

I remember the day I told the kids that I had cancer. I remember consulting with the psychologists and the social workers about what to say for kids at each age.

I remember that I prepared a page with the careful wording I wanted for each of them, so that I wouldn't get confused or forget the right way to say it, so I wouldn't forget the lines in the script of my life. I wanted to protect them at all cost, even though the content is scary and hard.

I was afraid I'd start crying in front of them, revealing my fear and I figured that if I stuck to the text and recited the words, I could, like a skilled actress, control my voice and my tone. Everything was so fresh and overwhelming but there was no time to wait and digest. The treatments had already been scheduled to start a week-and-a-half after receiving the diagnosis.

I'm amazed by how vivid that memory is, even though I've been through so much since then. Yotam's words in particular have stayed with me the whole way through: "I know that you will manage, and you will triumph, because you will do whatever it takes to get better. Even if it's hard and painful, you'll do it, so you'll win."

Yesterday the process came full circle when I sat him next to me on the couch in the living room and told him about the meeting I had with my "cancer doctor" that morning. I told him that the pathology report indicated that the cancer had been eliminated, and the happy bottom line: that as far as my doctor was concerned, I am healthy.

With the big smile and hug that I got from him in response, I added as we were hugging, "thank you for believing in me from the beginning, you believed that I would win."

And we did win, together.

I was surprised by his understated response. Maybe, like me, he was anxious and didn't want to start dancing for joy too quickly after the long months of uncertainty that we've been through. And maybe he just matured under the constraints of the illness, with the deep understanding that he demonstrated throughout. By contrast, Saar jumped at me with outstretched arms and cried happily, "Mommy doesn't have cancer anymore! Mommy doesn't have cancer anymore!" A second later he asked, "So now I can jump on you?"

Just like that, with one hugging me from either side, I explained to them that I still needed to recover from the surgery, and that in order to maintain my health and prevent the cancer from coming back, I would have to do radiation therapy and other, lighter treatments (our way of saying molecularly targeted therapy), which would occasionally make me tired or give me pain, but they wouldn't change the fact that I'm healthy.

It was important to me that they know that their mother was here to stay, and doing everything required, even if it was hard or painful, to go on winning, and to prevail, always.

August 1, 2018

Roller Coasters

After we got the news from the oncologist, we felt a powerful need to celebrate life. Assaf booked a flight and within two days we were sitting with the kids on a plane to Amsterdam, but the real destination was normalcy. We wanted to fly to a normal life.

It was so right for me, because the fact that we hadn't had time to plan the trip required that we make decisions on the move, which kept my head busy with attractions and routes and got the disease off my mind. I forgot a little of what I'd been through and it was just us, sticking together, as though trying to make up for the time we had missed.

The disconnection from the daily life of my illness was the real surgery.

The sharp transition from packing a hospital bag to packing a suitcase for a trip and from a schedule packed with medical tests and doctors to planning an itinerary for a trip abroad was like a dream. There were moments when it seemed to me that all the previous months had been a nightmare and that I had finally returned to reality.

On this trip I'm like a child. Everything is exciting, everything is special, everything is new.

Nobody knows me in Amsterdam. I take off my headscarf and reveal my sparse, cropped hair to the world, the healthy post-chemo sprouts of hair.

Upon landing in Amsterdam, we race towards Johan Cruyff Arena, the soccer stadium where Ajax plays, and we only reveal our destination to Yotam when we're already on our way there. According to their website, during the summer months, the last tour of the stadium is scheduled for 5 PM.

We get there, not before circling the entire, enormous stadium, trying to understand where the entrance is. All of that just to find that they have a mistake on the website, and that the last tour left at 4 PM.

Disappointment.

I try to convince the woman at the entrance to at least

let us see the stadium. I tell her that we had made the trip from one end of the city to the other immediately upon landing, to show Yotam a real European stadium.

But she just smiles politely and refuses, saying that they'll fire her if she does that.

We go outside and sit down on the steps. Saar and I rest and Assaf takes Yotam to the Ajax store, to soften the blow by shopping.

"Mommy, I have to pee," Saar tells me in his sweet voice.

At the same time, Assaf and Yotam return from the store. "Not interesting," says Yotam.

"I'll take him to the bathroom," Assaf takes Saar and marches back to the stadium lobby.

"I'm sorry it didn't work out, sweetheart," I say to Yotam with genuine dismay. I so wanted to do something special for him. Despite the perspective I have gained in recent months, my heart is full of sorrow.

"Maybe we can come here a different day?" he asks.

"I don't think that's likely because the stadium isn't on the way to any of the activities or plans we have for the next few days and it would have to be instead of some other activity," I explain.

Assaf and Saar come back through a swiveling door, Saar keeps going in our direction and Assaf suddenly sprints back inside without saying a word. I don't understand what's going on and follow him with my eyes to see what's happening in the transparent lobby. Yotam and Saar jump on the stairs and chat, and I notice Assaf gesturing to us to come quickly. I still don't know why, but I round up the kids and the three of us race over.

"When I was coming out with Saar, suddenly this guy came in with a red shirt that said 'Guide' on the back. I ran after him and asked him if he would be willing just to show us the stadium from inside so that we wouldn't disappoint the kids, and he agreed," Assaf smiles and his face beams with happiness at this plot twist.

"Dad talked with the nice guide and he agreed to let us in to see the stadium!" I lean toward the kids and tell them.

Yotam jumps with excitement and Saar joins in.

Like a mother goose, the guide walks ahead and the four of us follow him. We go up the stairs and he opens the stadium door beside the VIP area for us.

An enormous, resplendent stadium opens before us. The guide gestures for us to come in. It's much more than I thought he would do. We sit down in the VIP seats, taking photos with the stadium in the background and photographing Yotam and Saar making lots of faces in front of different backdrops.

I approach the guide and tell him: "Jewish culture has this concept of a 'mitzvah', which means doing a good deed for someone else. I want you to know that what you did here is a mitzvah. You made a little boy very happy. A little boy, who for the last eight months didn't get to go on any trips or outings, but rather had to be mindful of me while I was sick. And now we wanted to travel together and make him happy again. He was so disappointed that we'd missed the tour, and you managed to turn this day into a very special one for us, that we will always remember."

Now the guide gets excited, too, and says, "Thank you so much, I'm happy I could help."

Assaf and the kids thank him each in turn. "*Thank you, thank you,*" Yotam and Saar chant.

We leave happy, buy a Messi soccer ball for Yotam and a Barcelona one for Saar at a sports store, feeling a little like traitors, having just left Ajax's stadium, rivals of Barcelona. It was a good thing the guide wasn't there to catch us.

***

On this trip, it seems I'm only able to recall several moments, flashes of what actually happened in recent months. The rest of the time I have no free time to think. My head is full of trip plans and responsibilities and my eyes are full of new sights.

One morning, we are boarding the train on our way to the famous theme park, Efteling.

"There's a cow!" Saar shouts and points as we pass the green pastures.

"There's a windmill!" I point. "And another one!" And all of us are discovering the world anew, together.

We arrive to Efteling and rain pours down on us. We start running as a family to get under the awning at the entrance and sit there, protected from the rain.

Yotam spreads the map out and like an experienced general, he begins to point out where he wants to go.

"We'll start here, and then we'll go to this ride. We'll skip this next one and continue to the one after that. And then we've covered that zone and we can move on to the next zone."

"Sounds like a plan," we say in unison.

The rains stop and we invade the park. Assaf and Yotam get on the roller coaster in the dark while Saar and I wait for them. When they come out, smiling and full of adrenalin, Yotam pulls me to come with him for another round. Without thinking twice, I run with him hand in hand, excitedly to the ride, while Yotam tells me how fun and scary it is.

"It's really fast and then suddenly there's a drop and you don't even know where it goes because it's dark and then everything is a surprise, which is even more scary!" He shoots words at roller coaster speed.

Usually I was afraid of roller coasters. This time I wasn't. Everything he described sounded like the roller coaster I had been on over the past months; in the darkness of uncertainty, with the endless ups and downs - even the ups unpredictable and not less scary.

Our turn came. We got on and rode into the darkness, which, this time, was all fun and enjoyment.

August 12, 2018

Negatively Positive or Positively Negative

For three weeks now I've been walking around having a kind of identity crisis.

After a long period of months, which felt even longer to me, in which I breathed, stood, slept, ate and vomited cancer, months in which I was oncological, a cancer patient, one in nine, or one in eight as some would say — now I have difficulty understanding or figuring out who I am without cancer.

The treatments continue: targeted therapy, physiotherapy for my arm, and in two weeks I'll start radiation therapy. I visit the hospital frequently, coordinating appointments and doctors and treatments as though I was still ill. I sit in waiting rooms, alongside people with headscarves and face masks, and I am no longer one of them, but I still behave as though I am.

Does it make sense that it's so hard for the mind to disconnect from the illness?

The totality of that period was so powerful, so suffocating, that it doesn't leave room for light or air to enter and everything draws you into its depths like a black hole. I am still living in its gravitational field, not managing to disengage and shine like who I once was. I'm unable to feel healthy in my head and heart. Not internalizing it. When I try to shine and rejoice, the light always bends back in the direction of that black hole of cancer.

This weekend we celebrated the Bar Mitzvah of my sister's son. On Thursday morning he read from the Torah and his child's voice singing moved me deeply. Immediately, the dark thought crept into my mind that maybe I would not make it to Yotam and Saar's Bar Mitzvahs, because there are no promises in this life. Maybe I had this morbid thought because I had heard the day before that a popular inspirational speaker, who had recovered from metastatic breast cancer contrary to her doctor's predictions, had died suddenly at the age of 31 after her cancer returned.

That news fed my black hole. I tried to shake my head,

to physically cast off the thought. I'm not her; everyone is born with their own destiny. Still, I wanted a good life for her, healthy and full. It's hard for me to come to terms with the fact that a fighter like her is lost to us.

Will I ever be able to truly internalize my health, even though there is always the shadow of doubt, and you must look over your shoulder to see if the disease might return?

At the end of the ceremony, when everyone had gone outside, my father suggested to me to come into the hall with him and speak my mind. I have to admit that the disease cracked the faith that I'd had until then. My faith, like me, was damaged. With the complex relationship between me and God, I went into the hall alongside my dear father (may he have a good long life), closed my eyes, and when I tried to express what was in my heart in a whisper, I burst into tears. It was a mix of fear, gratitude, prayer, anger and hope. I hoped that God could read my heart even without me speaking. Who am I now? Sick? Well?

Currently or previously oncological? I am mostly at peace with health, but still broken from my illness.

RADIATION THERAPY

Everywhere I look
There is more than meets the eye
Among the treetops
I see the pale blue sky
Its glare is dazzling
And deceptive.
Which way from here?
Is this the right path?
Where will it lead me?
Between the tree trunks
I see varied shades of green
Trees too dense to escape through
But not too dense to reveal
The way out of the woods
Which way from here?
Is this the right path?
Where will it lead me?
Everywhere I look
There is more than meets the eye.

The Walk in the Forest, Henri Rousseau, 1844-1910

August 31, 2018

More Radiant than Ever

Since the kids' summer programs ended, summer break has been a concentrated kids-fest, mostly sweet, sometimes too much.

The combination of their vacation and my avoidance of the sun makes for a lot of time cooped up at home and inevitable moments when the house feels like a pressure cooker.

A moment before the steam escaped, vapors of memory arose from just a few months earlier when I was slumped in bed listening to them move through the house, every part of me just wanting to be with them. Now here I am, getting a double dose of togetherness for which I should be grateful. .

Amidst all that, radiation therapy began this week.

I didn't know what to expect on the first day; I didn't know anyone on the staff. In the radiotherapy waiting room, just like at the outpatient clinic, I sit and wait for my turn. Everyone else there is older than me and I find myself asking myself once again how it is that I drew this lottery ticket so young. Their glances seem to ask the same question. At the hospital, on the cancer ward, my short hair communicated that I had recently undergone chemo. Anywhere else I was just a cool chick or a mom having a midlife crisis who had cropped her hair or was about to enlist in the marines.

When they called me in, I entered a large room. It was spacious and freezing. Three members of the staff guided me into a lying position on the bed, arranging its height and my head placement. My new friend for the coming months awaited me — "the accelerator," as they called it on the ward. It's a robot with one arm that radiates and the other arm that absorbs radiation, intended to dance around me during our daily session. The ceiling was painted in shades of purple and green so that it would be interesting to look up at during the process, and pleasant music plays, drowning out the sounds of the accelerator as it circles around me. Meanwhile I try to learn its steps to understand when the dance will come to an end.

Each day of this week, the accelerator and I meet for our robotic dance, with each session becoming more precise for it and more relaxed for me. As the days pass, I begin making jokes with the staff about the music, lying nonchalantly on the bed, experienced, smiling. They leave the room to activate the radiation and as happy songs play in the background, I feel a sudden sense of distress building up, as though a flicker of understanding of what I've gone through radiates through me; what am I going through, and who will I be when I get through this?

I still don't know.

Tears threaten to burst out, but my accelerator doesn't see or stop. It is goal-oriented, continuing to circle around me burning cells as my brain burns with thoughts. Maybe I'm beginning to digest everything that has happened? After all, how can you be happy and cheerful when so many things will never return to the way they were? It has to hit me at some point, everything that has been lost.

The robot moves and I get up from the bed along with a cloud of unsolved thoughts, distancing myself and continuing to the reality of my life that awaits me at home.

On my way I meet an acquaintance who has been sick (metastatic) for a decade now but is in excellent shape physically and emotionally. She tells me happily about the trips she went on this summer and her desire to enjoy herself, since it is clear that she won't reach old age. As she speaks I just look at her face and see that she is at peace with her situation, which strikes me as so special, her tranquility, even though she doesn't know how many years she has left, even though she knows that she won't get old. As I say goodbye to her my heart hurts even though they assured me that they didn't radiate it.

I will never be rid of the fear of returning to the abyss of death. That is the shadow of cancer that can't be eliminated with chemo or removed by operation or burned by radiation.

It follows me like a grey cloud, and I need to learn to move it to see the light, to be more radiant than ever.

September 14, 2018
Jewish New Year

Taking Stock

I try not to be angry at you
For taking my good wishes,
Crumpling them up and throwing them away.
Nor did you honor the wishes of those around me.
It was hard but I beat you;
You didn't allow me a proper schedule with holidays and
workdays
Just a calendar full of treatment dates
I had no day, no night
I was not a mother
Nor a wife
Not a daughter
Nor sister

Nor friend.
How could you be so cruel to me?
You were supposed to be good
I welcomed you in a moment after my father was diag-
nosed with cancer
I had hoped you would let me rest a little
I thought I deserved it
Just to focus on my dear parents and help them
I thought they deserved it
Then you arrived fighting and chaotic
You decided to roll the dice
To toss them against stable ground,
Gamble on my life
Disfigure my peace
Embitter my days.
If this was some sick game of yours
To see me sick, then you won.
But don't get me wrong
Your victory was temporary
Just like you
Because I got through you stronger.
Amidst all the darkness you spilled
I found the bright spots that remained
Glittering like fireflies
And showing me the way out.

Today I stand strong before you
To bid you goodbye
To tell you that I will only take the good that grew
And I will uproot all the bad
And the weeds too.
Goodbye, passing year
Blessed be this coming year
A year in which I will put myself at the center,
Not forced by circumstance but propelled by choice
To rehabilitate my body and soul, to stand firm once more.
May this year bring only good and fulfill my blessings,
For me and for all of those I love.
Amen.

September 21, 2018

Getting to the roots

When I was 15, my aunt was diagnosed with breast cancer.

There wasn't a lot of information at that time and they didn't understand exactly what it meant. She was a truly special soul. My parents went to visit her regularly and insisted on not taking me, so that I would remember her full of life as she had been in better days.

One night I dreamed that I was alone at home and she came knocking on the door of our house. In my dream, I opened the door and her appearance frightened me. Her face was pale, and her hair was thin, shaggy, and glued to her scalp. She looked withered and weak — not at all like the strong woman I remembered. With all the childish strength I had, I tried to hide my revulsion from her and explain to her that Mom and Dad weren't home, but she was welcome to come in. I offered her something to drink.

She stayed on the doorstep and politely refused my offer.

"I just came to say hi," she said.

A day later, the ringing of the home phone woke me up at the crack of dawn and I answered it sleepily. I recognized the deep voice of my father's brother. "Tell your father that Aunt Zipporah is gone," he said.

"Gone where?" I asked as though I had left all my intellect back in bed.

"Tell him she's gone, he'll understand," he said and hung up.

I realize now how much they tried to protect me then. I was 15, I wasn't a child. But the fact is that my father was the youngest of his siblings, and I am the youngest of his daughters. His family was older, and he already had to bury a number of family members, while at the same time trying to protect me from death.

I don't know why I unconsciously kept her story so close to my heart, until at age 23, I began knocking on doctors' doors for routine checkups. Some of them let me in, appreciating my awareness while others asked what I was doing there at my young age and practically kicked me out of their offices.

"Come back when you're forty," one surgeon said, a

senior in her field. If I had listened to her, I wouldn't be here at age 40 to tell my story.

But I'm like bamboo running wild in a yard; I came back again and again, trembling in corridors, waiting for the good news to calm me down. In the years since, I found other doctors who saw things differently. They made sure to send me for an annual ultrasound.

I didn't go by the book. I was the book. And now that I have enough energy to be mad, I'm angry. I am mad that I should have detected it earlier.

Even though by the measure of time, my case would be considered early detection (only three months before I had my semi-annual checkup), according to the disease spread index and lymph node involvement — not by the book early detection. And that makes me so angry. After all, what could I have done apart from what I did? How could I have improved my situation?

When I was diagnosed, I immediately thought of my aunt, and I felt as close to her in her absence as I had when she was alive. Throughout the whole chemo period I thought of her, of what she must have undergone and thought, of her terrible suffering, and all I wanted was to go visit her grave.

This week that finally happened.

***

My father and I, now both cancer survivors, decided to visit the family burial plots together. I joked a little about how many of our relatives live in cemeteries these days. We went from grave to grave, grandmother, aunts, uncles, then grandma and grandpa from the other side of the family. We stopped at each grave and said a few words. Then my father told a childhood story that I'd never heard before about how his sister would wash his dirty little feet after running around the yard and fields barefoot. I was moved. What a special family I have.

From there we continued to another cemetery where my aunt, the heroine of this chapter, is buried. The cemetery there is serene with a kind of magic in the air. I stood there amazed by the scenery, breathing in the air and the pleasant quiet mixed with the supersonic dissonance of death.

I crouched down for a private talk with my aunt. I expressed my gratitude that thanks to her I had been on the lookout, and thanks to her I am here to stay.

I hope she saw us standing there with our eyes shining, evoking another childhood memory of mine, and a more distant one from my father. In the Jewish calendar's ten days of repentance, while most people connect with and talk to the world above, I connected with and spoke to the world below. A visit to my roots, six feet under.

October 17, 2018

Rub Me the Wrong Way

As though from the strangest beauty spa in the world, I emerge tanned from the "tanning machine" with second degree burns and have to rub an endless assortment of ointments on myself that are supposed to soothe, soften, cure and disinfect my burned skin.

Burns are a different kind of pain.

Burns in places that stretch and move, like my armpit and neck, are really unpleasant, especially while they're moving. So, I've taken on a kind of thuggish walk, with my arm at a distance from my body, and a robotic rotation of the whole body instead of just my head so it wouldn't hurt. All in all, I feel like a character from the movie "Terminator."

In jocular moments, I look at my chest, where my

breasts are intertwined like a yin and yang, and I hear
Michael Jackson's song in my head:

"It doesn't matter if you're black or white..."

I will probably shed the skin remaining on me anyway,
like a snake; this disease has you rebirth yourself.

Again and again.

From out of the ruins of the treatments I grow anew

And regrow

Skin and hair,

Eyebrows and eyelashes

I grow fingernails,

Red and white blood cells

That will keep me safe

From without and from within.

November 26, 2018

A Celebration of Light

On the first night of Hanukkah, 2017, our singing fills the living room. Our table is covered with cheerful menorahs that have waited a whole year to celebrate light once again within darkness, but the colorful candles don't burn nearly as hot as the hearts of my family. I recite the words, smiling at everyone, but my heart is as heavy as lead.

I had a biopsy just the day before. A breast cancer cloud hovers over my head like scary black smoke.

Eight days, night after night of lighting candles and playing with the dreidel, of light and family, of warmth and song, eight days of prayer.

Like the jug of oil from the Hanukkah tale, I, too, stayed lit up for eight days, despite the nerve-wracking uncertainty, not knowing if darkness would descend upon me. A day after the eighth candle, the results came in, the jug of oil ran out and my joy was extinguished.

It will be a few more days until I know how lucky I am, days that will pass with sadness and difficult thoughts, loaded conversations with God and the angel of death and many, many tears.

My biopsy report won me medals in the oncological department for exceptionally fast-spreading cancer.

"For you — nothing but the best," says the angel of death from the corner of the room with a half-smile and I am overwhelmed by thoughts of metastasis.

The triumph of light over darkness has to begin with a little focused light.

One particularly rainy afternoon, several days after receiving the biopsy results, I only barely hear the doctor over the phone, telling me that "there is no metastasis". There are more tears, this time of relief, like drops of happiness in an ocean of sadness.

The Hanukkah miracle, I thought, was that I discovered the cancer in time, that I paid attention to myself and that I didn't put off getting checked until later.

I can win this, I can heal, I can live.

Light begins with one candle.

Eight months passed from the moment of discovery until the pathology reports that declared that I am cancer-free. Like the eight candles of Hanukkah which were lit one after another like all eight months, I survived, one after the other. The more I moved forward on my path to health, the more the light from the candles grew stronger.

I am holding a report in my hands once again: this time a pathology report, and this time I have prevailed across all the statistics.

"For you — nothing but the best," I say to the angel of death who is shrinking in defeat in the corner of the room, hiding from all the light from my menorah of victory.

Today, I hear powerful singing. All at once I see, in my mind, all my friends who helped and supported me, standing together like a choir, as a wall of support, maybe also a defensive wall. Their singing is loud and joyful, full of power and courage, and penetrates right to the heart.

I stand before them, waving my hands in a big embrace, like a conductor of the choir that helped me to triumph over cancer.

Chemotherapy of Love

The community that evolved began as a result of our children's education. All the parents wanted more and so we gathered together. We went from being strangers to becoming an intimate community, whose interactions were the very essence of "good education," built on values, care, responsibility and love.

As time went on, I could feel the essence of this new community in my bones. I now have a circle of friends and acquaintances, parents from my sons' classes and members of our community that became a source of support and love as they held us close. Thanks to them I feel that we, as a family, are not alone in this rugged journey.

They wove a safety net for us, an entire army that stood

behind us, strengthened us while we were in motion, and were ready to catch us should we fall.

There were the ones that looked after my older son every day after school, took him in and gave him a feeling of security, friendship, and the chance to share what was on his mind.

The ones who stepped up to cook for us and relieve our burden, to pamper us and enable me to concentrate on the treatments, on resting, and having free time for myself.

The ones who surprised us with cake, sweets for the kids on the weekend, an empowering note, a craft project, or anything that came from the heart.

The ones who took an interest and were encouraging and accepting even on those days when I didn't have the strength or will to respond.

The ones who, with experience of their own, helped me put on a headscarf and create a look for myself that would be comfortable and pleasant, and at the same time accepted me without any of it, as I am.

The ones who took turns taking me out for some air to make me happy, going for a walk, putting on nail polish, doing creative activities, eating brunch.

That communal mobilization, with its power, its scope, and its essence, fills our hearts and envelops us.

In this world in which the feeling of isolation is getting more extreme, when people are increasingly motivated by their own interests, and egoism is on the rise, my supportive community is like an enclave of good-heartedness, a world in which there are still deep-rooted values of partnership, love of others, contribution and looking out for one another.

On one of the days during the chemo period, I was invited to a Sabbath ritual in which women of our community were present. When I received the invitation, I saw that the event was scheduled for two days after a treatment and I assumed that I wouldn't feel well enough to attend, even though I really wanted to. To my happy surprise, the side effects of that treatment were late in coming and allowed me to attend the event that evening.

That sense of female tribalism, the embrace, both physically and conversationally, the house full of love and femininity, and the true understanding of the meaning and responsibility of this difficult illness for me as a woman with a family, as a mother of small children — were uplifting.

I received a blessing for health from the women of my tribe. I was very moved and a little embarrassed. I don't like being the center of attention and I must admit that

I was also anxious about being seen in public without my hair for the first time. But I didn't want that evening to end. There was companionship and comfort, smiles and support, much sweet laughter, and a few bitter tears. There were blessings and a sense of holiness. There was a powerful female tribe, a feeling of home and family. A chemotherapy of love.

January 9, 2019

Cycles

A year —
A year has passed —
A whole revolution of the earth around the sun.
Visions of the starting point float before my eyes.
The first tests,
The biopsy,
The moment when we received the news,
The first day of chemo...

It's like traveling along a timeline whose starting point began on the day my life was struck by cancer and where each marker is a memory.

There is a great sadness within me when I think of the suffering that all of us went through, and also a detached feeling when I imagine myself as that weak, bald woman. The strangeness that I feel towards her is weird to me. Do I want to distance myself from her in my memory? Is distancing myself from her memory like distancing myself from the illness and suffering?

On this anniversary, there are many thoughts of this sort, of where I was then and where I am today, of the interminable fear of tomorrow.

Soon the slow disengagement from the hospital will begin. That process is mostly joyful but mixed with panic. The close connection to all the medical mechanisms on a daily basis gives me a sense of security, a firewall that will prevent **it** from returning to me. This disengagement puts the responsibility back on me to pay attention to every sensation and to decide what needs to be checked or monitored and what doesn't.

Apart from this hospital disengagement, I am experiencing a kind of push-pull relationship with my preoccupation with cancer. On the one hand, from the very beginning of my recovery, I saw the exciting mobilization of people in the network of patient support and I knew that I would want to do something like that when I recovered. On the other hand, remaining surrounded by the sick and in this sick environment feeds my fears.

Last week I was in the hospital for the day to get my

targeted therapy. I don't know how it happened that three women with breast cancer of the same kind (similar DNA) wound up in the same room.

All of us were waiting for similar medicine. The oldest among us was accompanied by her son. He asked us questions about the treatments, which galvanized a lively conversation. As the conversation deepened, the patient who was on her own turned to me and whispered to me that her cancer was metastatic. I don't know why she chose to whisper and why she thought she had to hide that information from the oldest and not the youngest patient in the room, for whom it has been a constant nightmare this past year. Of course, from that moment on I found myself dredging up every detail of our conversation and trying to piece together a picture in my head of her illness and the differences between the treatment she received and mine. I wanted to find as many differences as possible to prove that her "equation" was different than mine and so the result would be, too.

I returned home frightened, full of feelings. As though along with the infusion, the fears that had been hovering in that room had been infused in me too. I am not sure that I can describe that fear in words. She, however, seemed so calm, coming once every few weeks to get this drug, her lifeline, without which she wouldn't go on living. I don't know how it's possible to see, hear and know you're dying, but not let it affect you. I haven't found the formula for that yet.

I'm still searching for it.

February 25, 2019

The Woman from the Other Side

There's a bench on the hospital grounds that witnessed one of my relationship's toughest moments — a recitation of my last will and testament.

"If the treatments don't work," I told him, "if something goes wrong and it's the end of me," my voice shook, tears silently streamed down my pale, freezing skin, "I have two requests of you: First, I want you to move on with your life. Find new love, someone who will be good to you. Second, make sure she's good to the kids. I want them to grow up with a loving mother figure. They are so young and vulnerable, and they need a mom at their side." I was determined and didn't falter. "Promise me," I told him, despite the lump in my throat.

I look at that bench a lot. I remember that moment

and the doubt that fulfilling my second request would be possible. I realize that it wouldn't be easy to find someone who would want to raise kids that aren't hers, who would agree to take the place of their late mother.

As someone wise once told me — you can't compete with the dead. Despite their flaws, we always remember them as perfect.

Surprisingly, now, a year after that difficult conversation, when I'm healthy and on the mend, I met a woman who, in the name of love, was willing to take on children that are not hers, along with all of their hardships and frustrations of loss and death.

The details of her story mirror my own, only with the opposite outcome.

Her husband's first wife was diagnosed with breast cancer at age 37, she passed away at 40, and left behind children who were the same age as mine. Apart from the deep sadness I felt upon hearing this story, I experienced an incredible feeling of relief for the first time since that conversation on the bench. The very existence of this woman leads me to believe that there must be others like her — women who would take under their wings the children of a mother who had not survived her battle.

Those women that offer love must sometimes be pushed away by the children's pain and loss.

Those women that remain and want to be accepted, not as a replacement, but as a person.

Those women that plant their feet on the ground and strive to grow roots for the stability of the family.

Those special women.

March 18, 2019

Life Afterwards

If life during the disease was a roller coaster ride, life afterwards is like being on a swing.

There are days of worry and days of elation. Days of despondency and days of triumph. In addition to the female, hormonal moods, after a long bout of being medically suppressed, there are also post-oncological moods, because even when it's all over, it isn't really over.

Each doctor looks at you differently. Every back pain is a potential metastasis. Every protracted dizzy spell is grounds for a follow-up. Because there's the regular woman, and then there is the woman who had cancer.

There are those who want to join the ranks and support circles, volunteering to help people still struggling with the disease, and there are those who prefer to move on with their lives and try their best to ignore this chapter. I haven't decided which one I am yet.

Coming full circle, this year both Assaf and I attended Yotam's school's family day, to his great pleasure. The theme was giving, and we were asked to discuss the act of giving in the family.

"Tell him about the book," Assaf said to me.

I invited Yotam to come sit on my lap and said, "Do you remember how when I was sick, I wrote a blog about what we were going through?"

"Yes," he replied. He had seen me writing many times and asked me what the story was about.

"So, I thought it might help other women who found out they are sick to read a little about our journey so that they can be empowered by it."

Yotam smiled at me and I went on, "So, I'm planning to put it out as a book and give it as a gift to those women." I was moved and we hugged. Then, to my surprise, he asked if we could share that with everyone.

I had to overcome my embarrassment. Together, the two of us walked up to the microphone, before the crowd of class parents and the teaching staff, and we told them about my initiative. Yotam beamed with pride and I melted with the added benefit that my child was getting. What a meaningful lesson this is for all of us, to learn how, when life gives you lemons, to make lemonade.

Preserved Lemons

I spent many of my hardest days of the chemotherapy period sprawling on a lawn chair in my parents' yard, looking at their beautiful lemon tree and letting its fresh yellows and greens wash over all of cancer's pink and black that had taken over my life.

In one of the five biopsies I had, a nice doctor was treating me, and as he took a literal piece of me, he also gave me a piece of insight of his own. He smiled at us and said that after we finished this whole process and all the treatments, our family would come out the other side transformed; all of us would gain something from it and we would emerge stronger.

I was still very much at the beginning, in the stage of shock and numerous tests and checkups. It was a long time before I understood what he had seen happen many times before. It sounds a little cliché — to 'emerge stronger' — but now I realize that he was right.

Life gave me an enormous lemon tree and the choice to do what I wanted with it.

I could search for tiny pieces of happiness, like a sweetness in the pulp, and mix it with all that sourness to make a lemonade.

I could eat the lemons as they are and let their tartness embitter all my remaining days on earth.

I could do nothing, and waste away with them into rot.

Or I can do something else altogether. Press and squeeze the sadness and anger. Embrace the bitterness of the rind and the tartness of the pulp. Summon all these strong, powerful flavors and get through this bitter road, piece by piece.

What we have been through has compacted us together in this little jar of a disease. In the process, we have learned a life lesson, which we may otherwise have missed.

We are not here to let go. We came out of the process

changed, somehow softer with each other, but more resilient in everyday struggles and turmoil.

Better preserved.

Now we are a family of preserved lemons.

HEALED?

◆

Cancer is granted wide coverage for the many treatments, torments, success stories and their opposite. There is no one who has not heard or seen or does not know that cancer is not a simple illness and that to recover from it most people must undergo aggressive treatments.

This is precisely why we must talk about the moment after: after chemotherapy, after surgery, after radiation.

The moment after the illness, a moment that might be described as "healthy."

The moment the period of survival is over, the sense of relief is accompanied by the realization that this war is claiming lives, leaving scorched earth and real ruins of bodies and minds. It leaves impaired or partial functionality, a fragile mind and fear, a lot of fear.

Medical procedures leave lasting effects on the body, doing damage to the proper function of such critical systems as the nervous and lymphatic systems and the sensory systems such as vision and hearing. We are prohibited from lifting any load with the arm that was operated and radiated, an arm that once enabled us to lift our young children. The thought that we might no longer be able to lift them to us, not for a hug in a burst of love or to care for them when they are unwell, is a loss unto itself, more than the inability to tie their shoelaces or button their shirts. The scars and radiation burns on the body do damage to our self-image. We are left with muscle fatigue and reduced energy. But the page is too short to contain the extensive list of damages that we must re-learn to live with.

We may be healthy in the sense that we are free of cancer, but we are unwell regarding all the above. Certainly not as healthy as we were before.

As the storm of treatments and hospital-runs subsides, the glimmers of understanding suddenly emerge. Sometimes it feels weird as though until now I thought that someone else, not me, was going through all this and now that imaginary woman and I are beginning to merge in flashes. Every one of those flashes is painful and frightening and requires work on one's self and even professional help to deal with the difficulty and to digest something so big.

Would going back to past routines mean returning to being who I was? To carry on down the same road? After all, I'm no longer the same woman.

Cancer took away my innocence. From the first moment of contact between us, like a stain, or some mark of shame, I understand that we may meet again, that I have a higher likelihood than someone who has never encountered it. There will never be another bodily sensation that isn't shrouded in the fear of its return. There will be no more innocence or peace of mind, only fear, at times more repressed and at times less.

The soul is so full that any additional challenge in life just slides out; there is no capacity for anything else. Big or small. No ability to concentrate on anything in depth, only on routine actions, clear and certain, where the control is mine alone. No ability to learn, no patience.

Those who have not been through it would not

understand. The average person doesn't pay attention, doesn't give it a name and for the most part has no knowledge of it either, but it is real.

After we've treated the illness, the cancer, it is time to take care of one's self: a rehabilitation period.

Getting back up after a fall takes more time than the fall itself and healing from its wounds takes even longer.

The time has come to recognize that a rehabilitation period is necessary. Write about it in books, in research, in pamphlets. Write and discuss and acknowledge it in programs and organizations and institutions.

Do not let us apologize and justify ourselves for not being ready yet, do not make us feel like we're making excuses.

Our lives just got hit by a meteor, we need time.

Recipe for Preserved Lemon Spread

Ingredients:

- 4 - 5 medium sized lemons
- A pint jar (similar in diameter to the lemons)
- Half a cup of fine salt

Preparation:

- Wash the outside peel of the lemons well and dry them with a towel
- Slice them into pieces of about 1 cm thickness (put the ends of the lemon aside for use later)
- Put the half cup of fine salt in a bowl and dip the first slice of lemon into it on both sides, then lay it on the bottom of the jar. Dip the second piece in the salt on just one side and place it in the jar on top of the first

with the salted side up

- Repeat this process for all the round slices until you have filled the jar up to its neck
- Take the ends of the lemons and squeeze the juice out of them into the jar. Use about 3-4 lemon-ends (depending on the space between the neck of the jar and the lid) to compress all the stacked lemons so that the ends are on top, touching the lid and pressing the lemon slices down
- Close the jar and leave it at room temperature out of direct sunlight for at least a month
- Open the jar, remove the seeds, and grind the rest, including the peel, for a velvety, delicious preserved lemon spread

Acknowledgments

I wouldn't have survived this period without the whole army of people who were so generous and supportive.

To Assaf, the man beside me, who proved to me again and again what true love is made of.

To Yotam and Saar, my sweet boys, who were considerate and loving, hugging me, and believing in me the whole way through.

To my parents, who held my hand and taught me to walk once again in my life even when my legs failed me.

To Orit, my beloved sister, who did not for one moment lose sight of her optimism amidst the heaps of laundry and made sure to give the kids all the motherly hugs they needed.

To my dear in-laws who gave us strength all the way along.

To Shirley Ashkenazi, my best friend and soulmate, who accompanied me through the hardships of the body and soul.

To our friends and community, who made things better for us throughout this entire time, who volunteered to look after us, cook, make us happy, help with the kids, and did it all with love.

To the winning medical team:
To my oncologist, Professor Rinat Yerushalmi, for giving me my life back, my surgeon Dr. Ada Magen, who protected me from fear.

To Dr. Sagit Meshulam, an artist of healing scars and making the broken whole again.

To Dr. Pnina Dorfman for the understanding, the humanity, and the constant availability, which went above and beyond.

To the breast imaging team, my family at the hospital, you with the ultrasounds in your hands and the warmth in your hearts, with your understanding and approach to patients as people. Dr. Ahuva Grubstein, Dr. Itai Gadiel, Yael Pasternak Uziel and my dear beloved Dr. Yael Rapson, who took me under her wings and into the embrace of the breast imaging family, looked after me day and night and was a voice of reason.

To Orit Zemach, my amazing editor, who took in my words and my emotions with sensitivity, grace, and professionalism, and advised me patiently throughout the whole process of producing the book, and to Beni Carmi for introducing us.

Thanks to the eBookpro team for creating this book in English, allowing my story to reach so many people worldwide.

And if I have accidentally forgotten someone, I express my gratitude to you, too. My post-chemo memory is not what it used to be.

Yours, with love,
Ronit.

Sources

Beilinson Hospital has an art exhibition on display, courtesy of former Knesset member Mr. Samuel Plato-Sharon, of blessed memory.

Some of the artworks inspired me to write the poems in this book and they appear alongside those poems. The works are listed below in order of appearance:

Tiger in a Tropical Storm by Henri Rousseau, 1891
Source: WikiArt

In the Park of the Chateau Noir by Paul Cézanne, 1900
Source: WikiArt

The Hippopotamus and Crocodile Hunt by Peter Paul Rubens, 1615-1616
Source: WikiArt

War by Henri Rousseau, 1894
Source: Wikipedia

Mademoiselle V... in the Costume of an Espada by
Edouard Manet, 1862
Source: WikiArt

Garden at Sainte-Adresse by Claude Monet, 1867
Source: Wikipedia

Battle by Eugene Delacroix 1798-1863
Source: WikiArt

Woman Holding a Balance by Johannes Vermeer,
1662-1663
Source: Wikipedia

The Repast of the Lion by Henri Rousseau, 1907
Source: WikiArt

The Walk in the Forest by Henri Rousseau, 1844-1910
Source: WikiArt

Made in the USA
Coppell, TX
29 April 2021

54711723R00128